1001
Questions
& Answers

DORLING KINDERSLEY
London • New York • Stuttgart

Early theater tickets

A DORLING KINDERSLEY BOOK

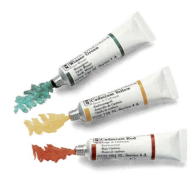

Tubes of colored paint

Written and edited by
Helena Spiteri and David Pickering
Art editor Diane Clouting
Design Susan St. Louis
Managing art editor Julia Harris
Managing editor Gillian Denton
Production Catherine Semark
Picture research Ola Rudowska
Editorial consultants Neil Ardley, Ted Hart,
Ann Kramer, Richard Platt, and Barbara Taylor

Ether inhaler

First American Edition, 1995
2 4 6 8 10 9 7 5 3 1

Published in the United States by
Dorling Kindersley Publishing, Inc.,
95 Madison Avenue
New York, New York 10016

Peruvian bag

Published in Great Britain by Dorling Kindersley Limited.
Distributed by Houghton Mifflin Company, Boston.

Architectural gargoyle

Library of Congress Cataloging-in-Publication Data

1,001 questions and answers. -- 1st American ed.
  p.   cm.
ISBN 0-7894-0205-X
1. Children's questions and answers. 2. Curiosities
and wonders--Juvenile literature.
AG195.A15   1995
031.02--dc20   95-14796
                                              CIP
                                               AC

Color reproduction by Colourscan, Singapore
Printed in Singapore by Toppan

Newton's telescope

A rat cleaning itself

Contents

2 compact discs

Tortoise beetle

Referee's whistle

15th-century woman

Prehistoric Life

Q1. Were all of today's different continents once one land mass?

Q2. How long did dinosaurs inhabit the Earth: about 65, 165, or 265 million years?

Ginkgo leaves

Animal life first started about 1 billion years ago (bya), when soft-bodied creatures lived in water. These forms of early life gave rise to fish with internal bony skeletons. The first amphibians that could walk and breathe on land evolved from the fish. In turn, reptiles evolved. Dinosaurs were reptiles. Just like today's lizards, they had scaly skin and laid eggs. Fossils (animals or plants preserved over millions of years) of prehistoric life give us the clues with which we can piece together the history of our planet.

Styracosaurus skull

Q14. Does *Styracosaurus* mean vampire lizard, spiked lizard, or horned hunter?

Q15. Did the blades jutting from this backbone support spikes, plates, or a skin sail?

Q3. What was the biggest development in plants in the age of the dinosaurs?

Q8. Which present-day man-eating creatures are near relatives of the dinosaurs?

Q9. When did dinosaurs become extinct: 35, 65, or 95 mya (million years ago)?

Turtle shell fossil

Q4. Is it true that the name dinosaur means "scaly hunter"?

Iguanodon hand

Q10. Which group of reptiles is the oldest: turtles, lizards, or snakes?

Q11. Which modern creature was *Iguanodon* named after?

Q5. How many horns did a *Triceratops* have on its head?

Q12. What do you call resin that has hardened over millions of years?

Q6. Was the name "dinosaur" coined in 1792, 1842, or 1892?

Q13. Was *Stegosaurus's* brain the size of a walnut, an apple, or a melon?

Ouranosaurus skeleton

Q7. Was the earliest known bird a *Pterosaur*, a *Pterodactyl*, or an *Archaeopteryx*?

Q16. *Hypselosaurus* was 39 ft (12 m) long. Was one of its eggs as long as 5, 25, or 55 hen's eggs?

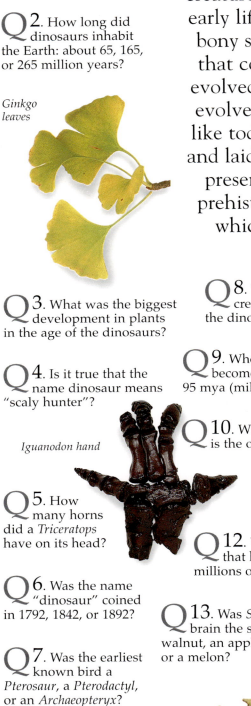

Q17. How big was *Hyracotherium*, the first horse: the size of a cat, a dog, or a deer?

Q18. How long did the prehistoric crocodile *Sarcosuchus* grow: 33 ft, 50 ft, or 66 ft (10 m, 15 m, or 20 m)?

Q25. The *Coelacanth* fish was discovered in the Indian Ocean in 1938. Why did it shock scientists?

Q26. How do we know what colors different dinosaurs were?

Q29. Which TV cartoon show (now also a film) features a prehistoric family?

Q30. What material from long-dead swamps fuels modern fires?

Q31. Why wouldn't cars move without fossils?

Q32. Can you name the hairy, elephantlike creatures that lived in prehistoric times?

Q33. India and Asia used to be separate land masses. What has been formed by their slow collision?

Q19. Is it true that dragonflies were flying through the skies 320 mya?

Q27. Were *Ouranosaurus*'s hands designed for attack or defense?

Q34. How many limbs does a tetrapod have?

Q20. Which dinosaur's name means "tyrant lizard"?

Q21. Which Steven Spielberg film featured dinosaurs recreated in the present day?

Fossil dragonfly

Q35. Was a dinosaur the biggest animal that has ever lived?

Q36. In which country have the most dinosaur remains been found?

Q22. Which flying "dinosaurs" had a 23-ft (7-m) wingspan: *Valdoraptors*, *Kronosaurs*, or *Pteranodons*?

Q28. Lucy is a 3-million-year-old woman whose remains were found in Ethiopia. Which pop song was she named after?

Q37. Is it true that prehistoric hippopotamuses were dug up under London's Trafalgar Square?

Q23. Did the prehistoric shark *Stethacanthus* have tiny teeth on its stomach, or on top of its head?

Q24. Was *Scelidosaurus* a meat eater or a plant eater?

Scelidosaurus

Reptiles

Q38. Which is the largest reptile in the world?

Q39. The longest-lived reptile on record was a tortoise: did it live to be 102, 152, or 202?

Q40. Is the snake to the left poisonous?

Sinaloan milksnake

Q41. Where does the most venomous snake in the world live: Africa, South America, or Australia?

Q42. Is the smallest reptile in the world 0.3 in (8 mm) long or 0.7 in (18 mm) long?

Q43. Human beings have 24 vertebrae. How many can a snake have: up to 200, 300, or 400?

Q44. Does the length of time snake eggs take to hatch vary with moisture or with temperature?

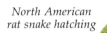

North American rat snake hatching

Q45. Which reptile features in Aesop's fable (story) about a race between the swift and the slow?

Q46. Is a stinkpot a kind of skunk, turtle, or lizard?

Madagascar day gecko

Q47. What is a Komodo dragon: a lizard, a turtle, or a snake?

Q48. Is a crocodile's stomach the size of a lunch box, a basketball, or an oil drum?

Q49. The tuatara of New Zealand is a unique lizard with a unique number of eyes. How many?

Crocodile

Q50. What do chameleons do?

Q51. Are reptiles warm-blooded?

Q52. The biggest turtle ever found weighed 2,120 lb (961 kg). Was it an African mud turtle, a snake-necked turtle, or a leatherback turtle?

Q53. Why does the sand lizard of the Namib desert "dance"?

Q54. Crocodiles, caimans, gharials – which members of the crocodile family are missing from this list?

Q55. Why are geckos often popular house guests?

Q56. Is the snake with the longest fangs a cobra, a viper, or a rattlesnake?

Starred tortoise

Q57. How long would a starred tortoise take to plod from one end of a soccer field to the other: 30 minutes, 45 minutes, or an hour?

Q58. Is the world reptile land-speed record holder a lizard or a snake?

Amphibians

Tadpoles

Q59. In one fairy tale a princess kisses a frog. What happens next?

Q60. How does the green toad keep enemies away?

Green toad

Q61. Do frogs lay their eggs in water or on land?

Q62. Is a caecilian an amphibian?

Frogspawn

Q63. Do frogs or toads usually have smooth, wet skin?

Q64. Why does a frog blink as it swallows?

Q65. Where does the male hip-pocket frog carry its tadpoles?

Q66. The most active known poison comes from the skin of South American golden poison-dart frogs. The poison from just one frog could kill: 500, 1,000, or 1,500 people?

Q67. Which children's story stars a toad who is friends with a mole, a rat, and a badger?

Q68. In legend, where did salamanders choose to make their homes?

Tiger salamander

Q69. What is a hellbender: a frog, a toad, or a salamander?

Q70. What do salamanders, newts, and sirens have that other amphibians do not?

Q71. How many mosquitoes can the dwarf puddle frog (which is the size of a large peanut) eat in one night: 60, 80, or 100?

Q72. How old are these tadpoles: 4 weeks, 6 weeks, or 8 weeks?

Q73. How do poison-dart frogs warn enemies that they are poisonous to eat?

Poison-dart frog

Q74. Which human divers are named after an amphibian?

Q75. Which television show starred a frog who was loved by a pig?

Q76. Is the largest frog in the world named after Goliath, Hercules, Atlas, or Godzilla?

Q77. The word "amphibian" comes from the Greek for "double-life." Why were amphibians given this name?

Q78. Is the world frog-jumping record 10 ft, 17 ft, or 23 ft (3 m, 5 m, or 7 m) for a single jump?

European common frog going after prey

Q79. Can all frogs leap?

Life in the Ocean

Q80. Is the fish to the left an angelfish or a parrot fish?

Q81. What is the largest wildlife habitat on Earth?

Q82. Which whale has a horn growing out of its forehead?

Q83. What kind of bulls swim in the sea and sometimes eat people?

Q84. Which whale has the largest brain?

Q85. What are a walrus's long tusks used for?

Q86. Which jellyfish gives the nastiest sting?

Q87. Most fish have internal skeletons made of bone. Are sharks' skeletons made of bone?

Q88. Are sea sponges animals or plants?

Graceful fish

Dolphin swimming sequence

Q89. Can seals sleep underwater?

Q90. How does a squid seize and kill its prey?

Q91. Which octopus is the most deadly?

Q92. Why do octopus, squid, and cuttlefish squirt clouds of ink?

Male seahorse

Q93. Which famous story by Lewis Carroll features a walrus?

Inflated pufferfish

Q94. Can some fish fly?

Q95. What is so unusual about a male seahorse?

Q96. Does a lobster have bones?

Q97. How much krill (tiny shrimplike creatures) does a blue whale eat each day: 4, 6, or 8 tons?

Q98. What do crabs do when they get too big for their shells?

Q99. What is the difference between a shark and a dolphin?

Q100. Is the shortest fish the Philippino dwarf pygmy goby or the minnow?

Q101. Which is the most ferocious freshwater fish?

Q102. How does a starfish feed itself?

Q103. Which fish can lay the most eggs: a sunfish, a clownfish, or a butterfly fish?

Q104. Which whale can hunt right onto the shore?

Q105. How does a ray hide from a hungry predator?

Q106. What do you call a group of fish swimming together?

Q107. Why is the beluga sturgeon such a valuable fish?

Q108. What keeps whales, walruses, seals, and sea lions so warm?

Q109. Why are sharks often called "primitive" creatures?

Q110. Why does the pufferfish inflate itself like a balloon?

Q111. Which sign of the zodiac is a fish?

Q112. Which fish can leap out of the water to catch prey: the archerfish or the anglerfish?

Q113. How long can the blue clam live: 10 years, 50 years, or 100 years?

Q114. Which fish can come onto land and breathe fresh air?

Q115. Which creature is longer: a sperm whale or a giant squid?

Q116. Is a dolphin a pinniped?

Great white shark

Q117. How many rows of teeth does a great white shark have?

Q118. Why does a catfish have whiskers?

Snakelocks anemone

Q119. Which fish has the longest snout: a swordfish or a saw shark?

Q120. How does the snakelocks anemone hunt and defend itself?

Q121. Which crab likes to move from one house to another?

Q122. What happens if you step on a stonefish?

Blue clam

Dogs

Q123. Which wolf is not a wolf?

Q134. How do dogs make the most of their height?

Side view of skull of bat-eared fox

An obedient Doberman

Sniffing beagle

Q130. Do foxes hunt in packs or on their own?

Q135. What is a dog's most highly developed sense?

Q124. There are more than 600 breeds of domestic dogs. True or false?

Q131. Which is the smallest member of the fox family: the fennec or the Arctic?

Q136. Which star do dogs look up to: Vega, Alpha Centauri, or Sirius?

Q125. If a dog's ears are laid back, what emotions might it be communicating?

Q132. Which dog is not a dog?

Q137. What is the most unusual feature of the maned wolf's body?

Q126. What is Mickey Mouse's dog's name?

Q127. Which is the most primitive breed of dog in the world: the dingo, the dachshund, or the deerhound?

Q138. What is a female fox called?

Q139. Why do bloodhounds wish they knew a good optometrist?

Dog leash and collar

Q140. According to legend, which two brothers were suckled by a she-wolf and founded a great city?

Q141. How old is this fox cub: 6 weeks, 10 weeks, or 14 weeks?

Fox cub

Q128. Who goes to work in a dog collar?

Q133. Which was the first dog in space: Lassie, Laika, or Lulu?

Maned wolf

Q129. Which famous Sherlock Holmes story is named after a dog?

Q142. What is the maximum area over which a pack of wolves will range: 40 sq miles (100 sq km), 200 sq miles (500 sq km), or 400 sq miles (1,000 sq km)?

Cats

A snoozing cat

Q143. How many hours a day do cats spend sleeping: 8, 12, or 16?

Q144. Which cat did the Greek hero Hercules kill?

Q145. Which is the fastest cat in the world?

Q146. Which cat has no tail?

Q147. Which cat did the author Rudyard Kipling write about?

Q148. What is the most obvious feature that distinguishes the lion from other cats?

Q149. Why do lions live in prides?

Q150. Which ones do most of the hunting in a pride: lions or lionesses?

Q151. Which is the only cat that can't retract its claws?

African male lion

Q152. Which poet wrote a book of poems about cats that has now been turned into the successful musical *Cats*?

Q153. Which sign of the zodiac is named after a cat?

Q154. Which cat can live without water for the longest time: a bobcat, a sand cat, or a tomcat?

Q155. Where was the first modern cat show held: London, Paris, or New York ?

Q156. Which are the biggest cats: tigers or lions?

A roaring leopard

Q157. What are black leopards better known as?

Q158. What would the Mochica people of Peru have done with this golden puma?

Golden puma

Bengal tiger

Q159. Which famous fictional, crafty, magical cat was created by Charles Perrault?

Q160. Can you name the fictional lion in C. S. Lewis's Narnia stories?

Q161. Which ancient civilization believed cats were sacred?

Q162. Do leopards roar?

Abyssinian cat

Q163. What is a cat's favorite plant?

Mammals

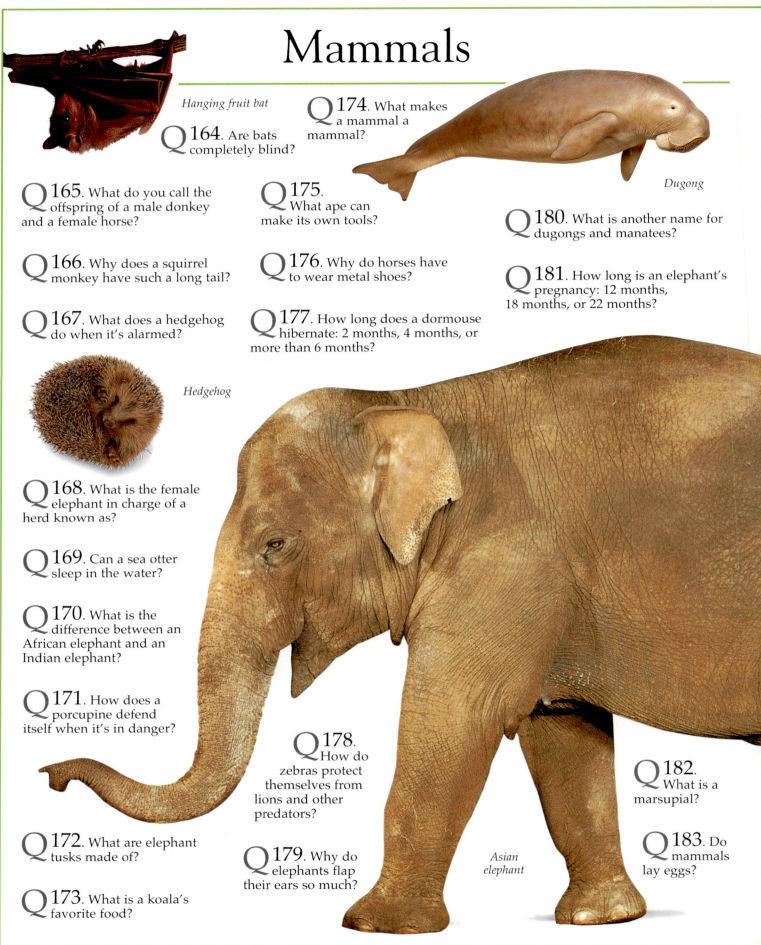

Hanging fruit bat

Q164. Are bats completely blind?

Q174. What makes a mammal a mammal?

Q165. What do you call the offspring of a male donkey and a female horse?

Q175. What ape can make its own tools?

Q166. Why does a squirrel monkey have such a long tail?

Q176. Why do horses have to wear metal shoes?

Q167. What does a hedgehog do when it's alarmed?

Q177. How long does a dormouse hibernate: 2 months, 4 months, or more than 6 months?

Hedgehog

Q168. What is the female elephant in charge of a herd known as?

Q169. Can a sea otter sleep in the water?

Q170. What is the difference between an African elephant and an Indian elephant?

Q171. How does a porcupine defend itself when it's in danger?

Q172. What are elephant tusks made of?

Q173. What is a koala's favorite food?

Dugong

Q180. What is another name for dugongs and manatees?

Q181. How long is an elephant's pregnancy: 12 months, 18 months, or 22 months?

Q178. How do zebras protect themselves from lions and other predators?

Q179. Why do elephants flap their ears so much?

Asian elephant

Q182. What is a marsupial?

Q183. Do mammals lay eggs?

12

Q184. In which continent would you find the small chinchilla rodent?

Q185. Which mammal lives, breeds, sleeps, and eats underground?

Rat cleaning itself

Palomino with Western-style bridle and saddle

Q186. How often can a female rat reproduce: every 4 weeks, every 6 weeks, or every 8 weeks?

Q197. Bats are the only mammals that can fly. True or false?

Sperm whale

Q198. In what do you measure a horse's height?

Q187. What does a herbivore eat?

Q188. What color was Moby Dick, the sperm whale in Herman Melville's novel?

Q199. What is a baby hare called?

Q200. What does a skunk do when it's attacked?

Q189. Which are more closely related to humans: apes or monkeys?

Q201. Which large, furry mammal spends all day hanging upside down in trees in the rain forests of South America?

Q190. Why are giant pandas in danger of becoming extinct?

Q191. Is a monkey a primate?

Q202. Which country has the most elephants: Zaire or Congo?

Q192. Who lives in a warren: a rat or a rabbit?

Q203. How do rams defend their territory?

Q193. Which is the smallest mammal?

Q204. Which is the largest deer: a moose or a caribou?

Q194. Why do some mammals like to groom each other?

Q205. Can bears swim?

Q195. How does a hamster store food?

Q206. What does a beaver build?

Q196. What are the 4 ways a horse moves?

Black bear

Q207. What color does a weasel's fur turn in snowy, cold climates?

Birds

Guillemot egg

American robin egg

Q208. Which bird lays the biggest eggs?

Q209. Is the bird with the most feathers an eagle, a swan, a duck, or an emu?

Q210. Which bird has "eyes" in its tail?

Q211. Why do some owls have one ear higher than the other?

Q212. The male sandgrouse can carry water 18 miles (30 km) across the desert for his chicks. Where does he store it?

Q213. Which lethal creatures does the long-legged secretary bird eat?

Q214. Does air flow faster above a bird's wing or below it?

Wing of shoveler duck

Q215. How fast can a hummingbird's wings beat: 60, 90, or 120 times a second?

Q216. How high can a bird fly: up to 7, 9, or 11 miles high (11, 14, or 17 km)?

Q217. Cave swiftlets make their nests with a material from their own bodies. Is it dung, silk, or saliva?

Redstart's nest

Lanner falcon

Q218. The fastest living creature is a falcon. Which falcon is it?

Q219. One kind of bird can remain in the air continuously for up to 10 years. Is it an albatross, a tern, or a skimmer?

Q220. One species of bird probably sees more daylight than any other creature. Is it the gyrfalcon, the storm petrel, or the Arctic tern?

Q221. Which bird of which colour is a symbol of peace?

Q222. Does a robin's heart beat 400, 500, or 600 times a minute?

Q223. Is the bird with the longest bill a stork, a pelican, a penguin, or a woodpecker?

Q224. Which is the world's smallest bird: the amethyst woodstar, or the bee hummingbird?

Q225. In Greek myth, was it Icarus or Achilles who flew too close to the sun?

Q226. Is it the emperor, king, or gentoo male penguin that incubates its eggs on its feet through the world's worst winter, in Antarctica?

Q227. In 1814 the passenger pigeon population was in the billions. In 1914, how many were left?

Q228. Are most birds' bones hollow or solid?

Q229. Is the bird with the greatest wingspan an eagle, a condor, or an albatross?

Bird skeleton

Q230. What makes the wrybill unique?

Mini-beasts

Q231. The Kayapo Indians of Brazil model their society on an insect that they think lives in perfect harmony. Which insect is it?

Q232. How many pairs of shoes would an arachnid need?

Tortoise beetle

Q233. Which beetles "fire a gun": dung, camphor, or bombardier beetles?

Q234. One particular kind of weevil has a very long neck. What is it called?

Q235. In which country would you find the world's most venomous spider: Australia, China, or Brazil?

Bumblebee

Q236. Are worker bees male or female?

Q237. The sun spiders of Africa and the Middle East are arachnid world record holders. Is their world record for size, speed, or reproduction?

Madagascan moon moth

Goliath beetle

Q245. What do caterpillars turn into when they grow up?

Earthworm

Q238. In the first World Worm Charming Championship, in 1980, competitors had 30 minutes to charm worms by vibrating a garden tool in the soil. Did the winner charm 311, 511, or 711 worms?

Peacock butterfly

Q239. Which luxury clothing material is made by moths?

Q240. For its size, the rhinoceros beetle is perhaps the world's strongest creature. Can it support 250, 550, or 850 times its own weight on its back?

Gold beetle

Q241. Why are moths attracted to bright lights?

Q242. Is the smallest spider 0.1, 0.06, or 0.02 in long (2.4, 1.4, or 0.4 mm)?

Q243. Are Goliath beetles or elephant beetles the largest of all beetles?

Brimstone butterfly

Q244. This butterfly has a hidden pattern on its wings. What kind of light would make that pattern show up?

Q246. Nephila spiders' webs are very strong. Are they used to make ropes, rugs, or fishing nets?

Q247. Why do glow worms glow?

Crab spider

Q248. What was the distance around the largest spider's web ever measured: 13, 20, or 27 ft (4, 6, or 8 m)?

Flowers and Plants

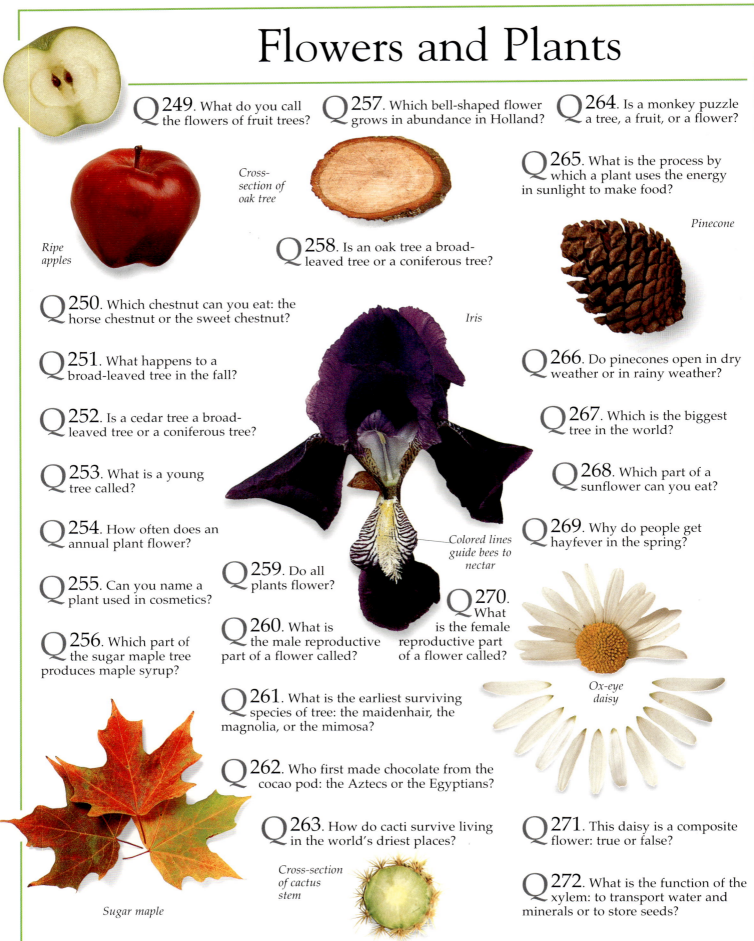

Q249. What do you call the flowers of fruit trees?

Q257. Which bell-shaped flower grows in abundance in Holland?

Q264. Is a monkey puzzle a tree, a fruit, or a flower?

Q265. What is the process by which a plant uses the energy in sunlight to make food?

Ripe apples

Cross-section of oak tree

Q258. Is an oak tree a broad-leaved tree or a coniferous tree?

Pinecone

Q250. Which chestnut can you eat: the horse chestnut or the sweet chestnut?

Q251. What happens to a broad-leaved tree in the fall?

Q252. Is a cedar tree a broad-leaved tree or a coniferous tree?

Q253. What is a young tree called?

Q254. How often does an annual plant flower?

Q255. Can you name a plant used in cosmetics?

Q256. Which part of the sugar maple tree produces maple syrup?

Iris

Q259. Do all plants flower?

Q260. What is the male reproductive part of a flower called?

Q261. What is the earliest surviving species of tree: the maidenhair, the magnolia, or the mimosa?

Q262. Who first made chocolate from the cocao pod: the Aztecs or the Egyptians?

Q263. How do cacti survive living in the world's driest places?

Colored lines guide bees to nectar

Q270. What is the female reproductive part of a flower called?

Q266. Do pinecones open in dry weather or in rainy weather?

Q267. Which is the biggest tree in the world?

Q268. Which part of a sunflower can you eat?

Q269. Why do people get hayfever in the spring?

Ox-eye daisy

Q271. This daisy is a composite flower: true or false?

Q272. What is the function of the xylem: to transport water and minerals or to store seeds?

Cross-section of cactus stem

Sugar maple

Parts of a flower

Q Can you identify the parts of this sunflower?

Sunflower

292.

293.

294.

295.

296.

Longitudinal section through a sunflower

Pink aster

Q273. What is pollination?

Q274. Where does the aster above most commonly grow: in deserts, by the seashore, or in fields?

Q275. What is the largest flower in the plant kingdom?

Daffodil

Q276. What is nectar?

Q278. What do you call the sticky sap that oozes out of coniferous trees?

Q279. What is the green pigment in leaves called?

Japanese maple leaf

Q277. What happens to a flower once it has been pollinated?

Lily flower

Q280. How is pollen carried from the male part to the female part of a flower?

Q281. What is the difference between a simple leaf and a compound leaf?

Q282. Do flowers smell strongest by day or by night?

Fly agaric mushroom

Q283. Does this mushroom help the trees it grows beside?

Q284. How can a plant protect itself from being eaten by a hungry animal?

Q285. What is a virgin forest?

Q286. Which tree produces acorns?

Acorns

Q287. Which plant bulb is supposed to keep vampires away?

Q288. Who was the Greek god of forests and flocks?

Q289. Can some plants eat insects?

Gerbera flower

Q290. How do you estimate the age of a tree?

Q291. Why are flowers so brightly colored?

Ancient Egypt

Mummy case of the lady Takhenmes

Understanding the past enriches our lives, and no part of history is more fascinating than the story of the land of the pyramids. The treasures of Egypt were ancient when Rome was a village, and they still inspire the world's wonder. As one proverb says, "Time laughs at all things, but the pyramids laugh at time."

Statue of priest

Q297. What was a mummy in ancient Egypt?

Q298. Who were the pharaohs?

Q299. One part of the god Horus's body became a symbol of protection. Was it his hand, his heart, or his eye?

Q300. Was the Egyptian Book of the Dead a collection of spells or a list of past pharaohs?

Q301. The Egyptians did not have paper. Did they use parchment or papyrus instead?

Q302. Can you name the lion with the head of a man that guards the way to King Khafra's pyramid at Giza?

Q303. Were the pharaohs buried on the west side of the Nile, or the east side?

Q305. Was Taweret, the goddess of childbirth, shown as a pregnant hippopotamus, stork, or cat?

Bracelet showing the god Horus

Q308. Was the scarab, or dung, beetle a symbol of the Sun god or the god of the underworld?

Q309. Was the sky goddess called Fruit or Nut?

Q304. Why did Egyptian priests shave their heads?

Q306. What was the longest any pharaoh reigned: 74, 84, or 94 years?

Q307. Why were the pyramids built?

Q310. Can you name the only pharaoh whose tomb escaped robbery in ancient times?

Q311. In ancient Egypt, did the ankh represent life, love, or the Sun?

Q312. Does this snake represent the cobra goddess or the python goddess?

The ankh, a powerful Egyptian symbol

Q313. Which legendary woman, famous for her beauty and fatal charm, was the last queen of Egypt before the Romans took over?

The pyramids at Giza

Statue of Pharaoh Senusret III

Q314. The Great Pyramid is one of the Seven Wonders of the ancient world. How much do all the stones in it weigh: 6.1, 7.2, or 8.3 million tons?

Q315. Was the god of long life called Heh, Neh, or Yeh?

Q316. Were Egyptian shoes usually made from leather or reeds?

Q317. Why were ibises mummified?

Mummy of an ibis

Q318. The Egyptians called part of their country "the black land" and part "the red land." Which part did they live in?

Q319. Why did Egyptians shave their eyebrows: as a mark of fashion, joy, or mourning?

Q320. Was senet a drink, a game, or a religious duty?

Q321. Were Egyptian clothes usually made from wool, cotton, nylon, or linen?

Q322. After the end of pyramid-building, in which valley were the kings of Egypt buried?

Q323. In an Egyptian calendar, was a red-letter day lucky or unlucky?

Q324. Is the Great Pyramid taller than England's St. Paul's Cathedral?

Q325. What were hieroglyphics?

Ancient Greece

Q326. For which god were the ancient Olympic Games held?

Q327. Is the famous port in Athens that has been used for 2,500 years called Piraeus, Plymouth, or Pompeii?

Q328. What were Greek soldiers called?

Well-preserved Greek coin

Q329. What mythological flying horse does this coin depict?

Q330. Who was Asclepiades: a doctor, a playwright, or a god?

Q331. What might a Greek citizen do at the agora?

Child's rattle shaped like a pig

Q332. What did Greek children do with their toys when they reached puberty?

Q333. Of whom was it said that her face had launched a thousand ships: the goddess Athena, Helen of Troy, or Queen Boudicca?

Clay jug and coins dating from 650–625 BC

Q334. What was a symposium?

Q335. What are these coins made of: gold, silver, or electrum?

Greek soldier

Decorated capital

Q336. Where in a building would you find this capital: on the roof, on top of a column, or above a doorway?

Q337. Can you name the legendary monster that was half-man, half-bull, and was killed by the young prince Theseus?

Q338. What was a trireme?

Drinking cup

Q339. Which was the Greeks' favorite drink: water, wine, or milk?

Q340. Which Athenian temple, dedicated to the goddess Athena, occupies the highest point of the Acropolis?

Q341. Who wrote the great epic poem the *Iliad*?

Q342. The Romans called him Neptune. What did the Greeks call him?

Q343. What political system first developed in Athens in the 5th century BC?

Ancient Rome

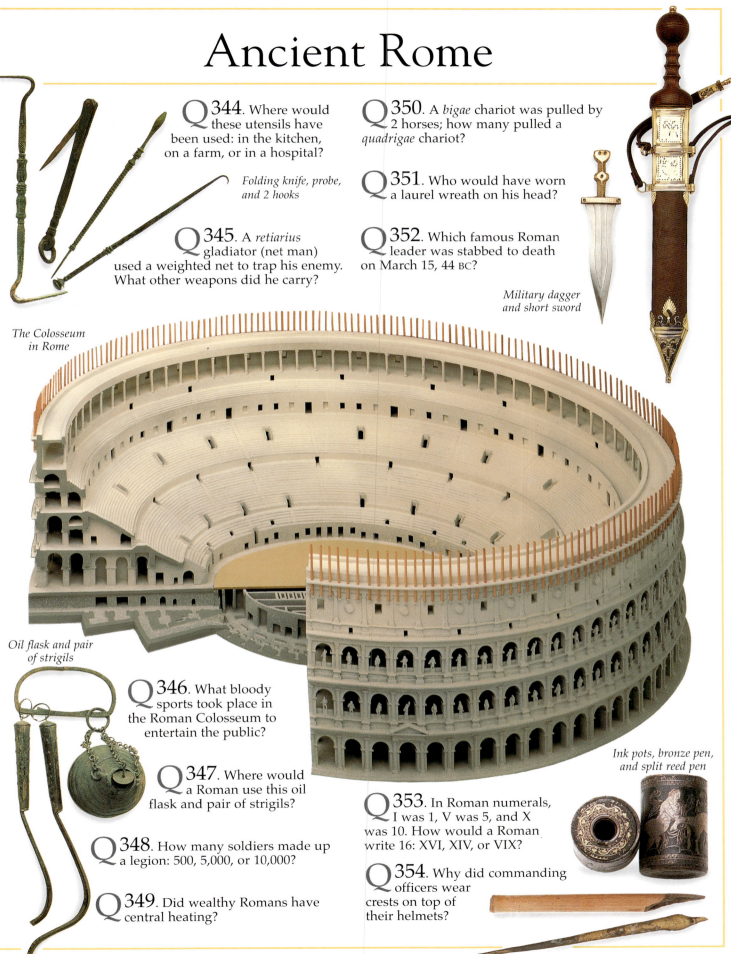

Q344. Where would these utensils have been used: in the kitchen, on a farm, or in a hospital?

Folding knife, probe, and 2 hooks

Q345. A *retiarius* gladiator (net man) used a weighted net to trap his enemy. What other weapons did he carry?

Q350. A *bigae* chariot was pulled by 2 horses; how many pulled a *quadrigae* chariot?

Q351. Who would have worn a laurel wreath on his head?

Q352. Which famous Roman leader was stabbed to death on March 15, 44 BC?

Military dagger and short sword

The Colosseum in Rome

Oil flask and pair of strigils

Q346. What bloody sports took place in the Roman Colosseum to entertain the public?

Q347. Where would a Roman use this oil flask and pair of strigils?

Q348. How many soldiers made up a legion: 500, 5,000, or 10,000?

Q349. Did wealthy Romans have central heating?

Ink pots, bronze pen, and split reed pen

Q353. In Roman numerals, I was 1, V was 5, and X was 10. How would a Roman write 16: XVI, XIV, or VIX?

Q354. Why did commanding officers wear crests on top of their helmets?

Medieval Life

Minstrel (musician)

Q355. Which legendary character, with his "merrie men," stole from the rich to give to the poor?

Q356. Who or what would have worn this pendant?

Q357. Was a flesh-hook used on a battlefield, in a kitchen, or in a graveyard?

Q358. Is this woman's dress called a kirtle or a skirtle?

15th-century woman

Q359. In which century did hand knitting begin in Europe: the 9th, 12th, or 15th?

Bodiam Castle in England

Q360. What is the ditch around a castle called?

Q361. Which were easier to defend: round towers or square towers?

Q362. Was a morning star a weapon or a decoration?

Q363. The name of this instrument is the name of its parts. What is it called?

Q364. Was a villein a villain?

Q365. In which country did Joan of Arc live?

Q366. Was pannage a tax on pans, a duty on beer, or the right to pasture pigs in a forest?

Pendant showing coat of arms

Q367. What is the keep of a castle?

Q368. What was the Black Death?

Q369. Were pigs sometimes trained as war hounds or as retrievers for use in hunting?

Q370. What was an apprentice knight before he "won his spurs"?

Q371. What is this armor designed to protect?

Q372. What did a knight throw on the ground to issue a challenge?

Q373. Was a castle's outer wall called the ring wall or the curtain wall?

Q374. From which flower did the English civil wars of the 1400s take their name?

Q375. In the 10th century King Wenceslaus ruled Bohemia in the Czech Republic. When is he remembered in song?

Q376. In the 1300s, which sport got in the way of archery practice and was banned by the king of England?

Q377. What were the Crusades?

Q378. What are samite, damask, and taffeta?

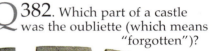

Crossbow

Q380. Who had to shoot an apple from his own son's head with a crossbow?

Q381. Comedians known as jesters used to slap people with a bladder on a stick. What was this called?

Q382. Which part of a castle was the oubliette (which means "forgotten")?

Q379. Why do these machicolations (overhanging battlements) have holes in their floors?

Shaffron armor

Renaissance

Q383. What is this young man's jacket called: a cravat, a doublet, or a stomacher?

Q384. In which Italian city-state did the Renaissance begin: Florence, Milan, or Venice?

Q385. What does the word Renaissance mean?

Fashionable Renaissance style

Q386. Is this woman's dress made of silk, velvet, or serge?

Q387. Which scholar challenged the view that the Earth was at the center of the Universe: Nicholaus Copernicus, Hans Lippershey, or Roger Bacon?

Q388. Which ancient civilization was a vital inspiration for the Renaissance?

Shield probably belonging to Charles V

Q389. Which noble family did Charles V belong to: the Hapsburgs, Tudors, or Romanovs?

Q390. Why was the 16th-century religious movement led by Martin Luther known as the Reformation?

Woman in 15th-century dress

Q391. Which great Renaissance artist and scientist designed an early tank and a flying machine?

Q392. Which 16th-century English queen owned these gloves?

Gloves belonging to a queen

Q393. Which Italian banking family used their money and influence to sponsor artists?

Q394. Can you name the romantic tragedy by William Shakespeare that was set in Verona: *Macbeth* or *Romeo and Juliet*?

An early printing press

Q395. The invention of the printing press by Johannes Gutenberg in 1450 enabled books to be mass-produced. In which country was it invented?

Q396. The Bible was the first book printed on Gutenberg's printing press. In which language was it written?

Gutenberg's Bible

Exploration

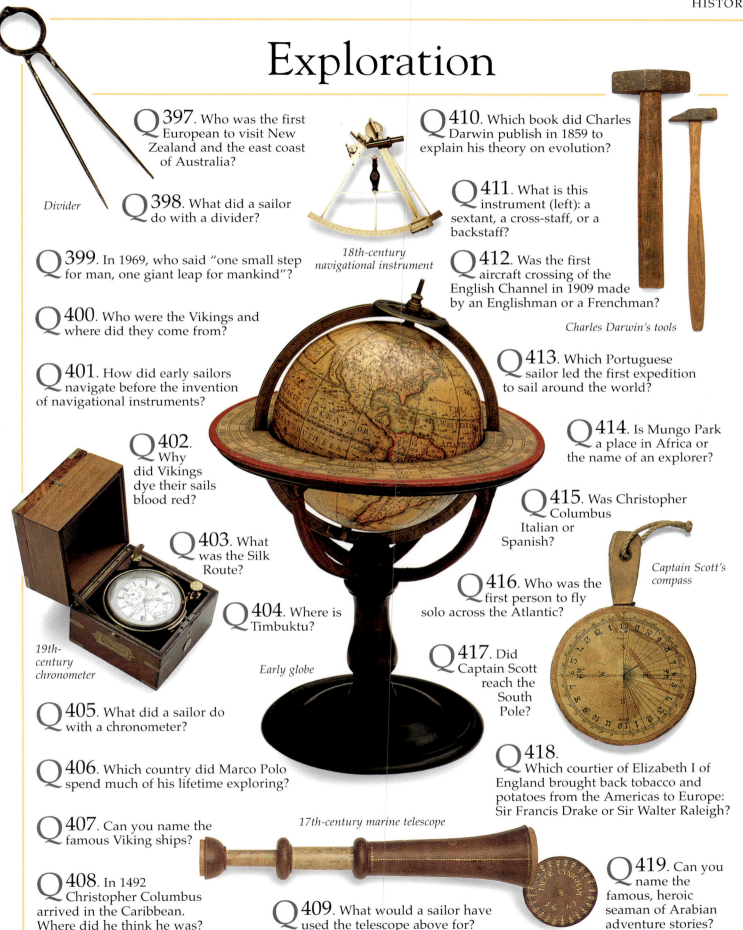

Q397. Who was the first European to visit New Zealand and the east coast of Australia?

Divider

Q398. What did a sailor do with a divider?

Q399. In 1969, who said "one small step for man, one giant leap for mankind"?

Q400. Who were the Vikings and where did they come from?

Q401. How did early sailors navigate before the invention of navigational instruments?

Q402. Why did Vikings dye their sails blood red?

Q403. What was the Silk Route?

Q404. Where is Timbuktu?

19th-century chronometer

Q405. What did a sailor do with a chronometer?

Q406. Which country did Marco Polo spend much of his lifetime exploring?

Q407. Can you name the famous Viking ships?

Q408. In 1492 Christopher Columbus arrived in the Caribbean. Where did he think he was?

Early globe

18th-century navigational instrument

Q410. Which book did Charles Darwin publish in 1859 to explain his theory on evolution?

Q411. What is this instrument (left): a sextant, a cross-staff, or a backstaff?

Q412. Was the first aircraft crossing of the English Channel in 1909 made by an Englishman or a Frenchman?

Charles Darwin's tools

Q413. Which Portuguese sailor led the first expedition to sail around the world?

Q414. Is Mungo Park a place in Africa or the name of an explorer?

Q415. Was Christopher Columbus Italian or Spanish?

Q416. Who was the first person to fly solo across the Atlantic?

Captain Scott's compass

Q417. Did Captain Scott reach the South Pole?

Q418. Which courtier of Elizabeth I of England brought back tobacco and potatoes from the Americas to Europe: Sir Francis Drake or Sir Walter Raleigh?

17th-century marine telescope

Q409. What would a sailor have used the telescope above for?

Q419. Can you name the famous, heroic seaman of Arabian adventure stories?

Aztecs and Incas

Teotihuacan mask

Q420. Which method of sacrifice did the Maya think was right for their rain god?

Q421. Turquoise, coral, shell, obsidian, silver: which of these materials does not appear in the mask above?

Q422. Who lived in "the World of the Fifth Sun"?

Q423. Was Tlaloc the Aztec god of rain or the Aztec god of war?

Water vessel of Aztec god Tlaloc

Q424. Whose elite warriors were named after the jaguar and the eagle?

Q425. Which animal did the Incas use for transportation?

Q426. Which invention, *very* useful for transportation, did the Incas fail to use?

Q427. Were the Aztecs' "Wars of Flowers" fought for flowers or prisoners?

Nazca textile

Q428. In ancient Peru, did men or women carry bags like this, used to carry coca leaves and amulets (good luck charms)?

Q429. Who is Mexico named after?

Q430. Did the Nazca people live in Mexico or Peru?

Maya rain god, Chac

Q431. From which animal does the skin on this shield come?

Aztec shield

Q432. Did the Aztecs pay taxes to chinampas, grow crops on them, or fill them with chilies and eat them?

Q433. In 1519 Spanish conquistadors arrived in Mexico on animals that the Aztecs had never seen before. What were they?

Q434. Are tomatoes, peanuts, pineapples, and sweet potatoes native to Europe or the Americas?

Peruvian bag

Q435. How was the Aztec capital, Tenochtitlan, like Venice?

Q436. In 1500, which was bigger: Tenochtitlan or London, England?

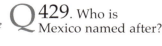

The Wild West

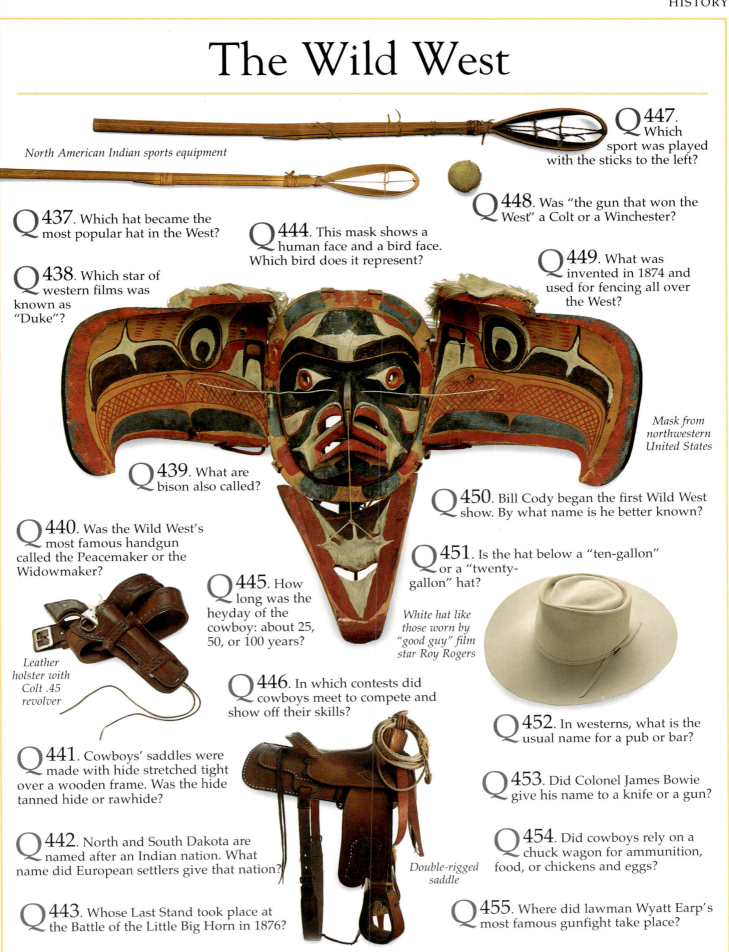

North American Indian sports equipment

Q447. Which sport was played with the sticks to the left?

Q448. Was "the gun that won the West" a Colt or a Winchester?

Q437. Which hat became the most popular hat in the West?

Q444. This mask shows a human face and a bird face. Which bird does it represent?

Q449. What was invented in 1874 and used for fencing all over the West?

Q438. Which star of western films was known as "Duke"?

Mask from northwestern United States

Q439. What are bison also called?

Q450. Bill Cody began the first Wild West show. By what name is he better known?

Q440. Was the Wild West's most famous handgun called the Peacemaker or the Widowmaker?

Q451. Is the hat below a "ten-gallon" or a "twenty-gallon" hat?

Q445. How long was the heyday of the cowboy: about 25, 50, or 100 years?

White hat like those worn by "good guy" film star Roy Rogers

Leather holster with Colt .45 revolver

Q446. In which contests did cowboys meet to compete and show off their skills?

Q452. In westerns, what is the usual name for a pub or bar?

Q441. Cowboys' saddles were made with hide stretched tight over a wooden frame. Was the hide tanned hide or rawhide?

Q453. Did Colonel James Bowie give his name to a knife or a gun?

Q442. North and South Dakota are named after an Indian nation. What name did European settlers give that nation?

Q454. Did cowboys rely on a chuck wagon for ammunition, food, or chickens and eggs?

Double-rigged saddle

Q443. Whose Last Stand took place at the Battle of the Little Big Horn in 1876?

Q455. Where did lawman Wyatt Earp's most famous gunfight take place?

Weaponry and War

Q456. What kind of hairy and non-military feature did General Ambrose Burnside give his name to?

Q457. Where did the largest invasion of all time take place on D-day (6 June, 1944)?

Q458. Is a scimitar a straight or a curved sword?

17th-century sword

Q459. Which can fire an arrow farther: a crossbow or a longbow?

Q460. Is the sword above a smallsword, a backsword, or a hunting sword?

Q461. From what kind of metal are bullets traditionally made?

Gun bullets

Q462. How many soldiers made up the gun crew of this cannon: about 2, 5, or 10?

Q463. How many shots could you fire from this revolver without reloading: 5, 8, or 10?

Colt police revolver

Q464. Was a musket a gun or a shield?

Q465. Dugouts are a feature of modern warfare. What are they?

Muzzle-loading cannon

Q466. In World War II, what was a U-boat?

Q467. Who led elephants across the Alps and won many battles against Rome, although in the end he lost the war?

Q468. What was the last big sea battle waged between German and British fleets: Jutland, Trafalgar, or Pearl Harbor?

Q469. He seemed invincible in battle, he crowned himself emperor of France, but in the end he was defeated at Waterloo and exiled. Who was he?

Hand-ax

Q470. What is this hand-ax made of?

Q471. Which fighting machine first rumbled into action on the battlefields of World War I?

Zulu Spear

Q472. In an army, which of these is the most senior in rank: a colonel, a captain, or a corporal?

Q473. What was the most important weapon carried by a samurai warrior?

Q474. Is an AK47 a gun, a tank, or a missile?

Q475. Is this spear designed for throwing or for thrusting?

Q476. When grenades were first used in Europe, what were the troops who were trained to use them called?

Q477. What was this nasty looking object used for?

A caltrop

28

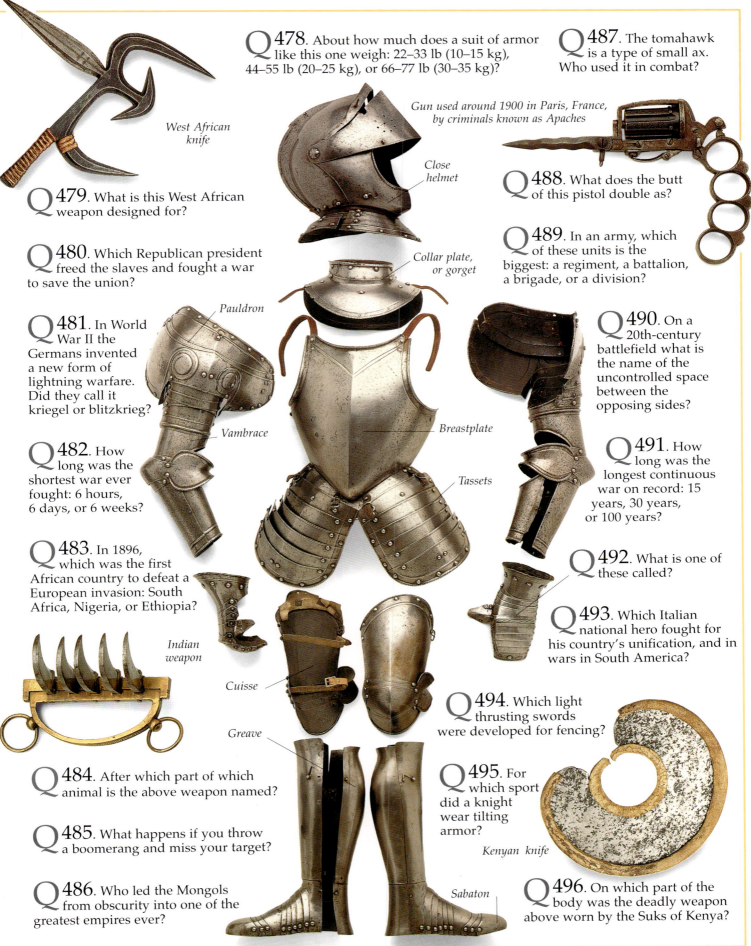

West African knife

Q478. About how much does a suit of armor like this one weigh: 22–33 lb (10–15 kg), 44–55 lb (20–25 kg), or 66–77 lb (30–35 kg)?

Gun used around 1900 in Paris, France, by criminals known as Apaches

Close helmet

Q487. The tomahawk is a type of small ax. Who used it in combat?

Q479. What is this West African weapon designed for?

Q480. Which Republican president freed the slaves and fought a war to save the union?

Collar plate, or gorget

Q488. What does the butt of this pistol double as?

Q489. In an army, which of these units is the biggest: a regiment, a battalion, a brigade, or a division?

Pauldron

Q481. In World War II the Germans invented a new form of lightning warfare. Did they call it kriegel or blitzkrieg?

Vambrace

Breastplate

Q490. On a 20th-century battlefield what is the name of the uncontrolled space between the opposing sides?

Q482. How long was the shortest war ever fought: 6 hours, 6 days, or 6 weeks?

Tassets

Q491. How long was the longest continuous war on record: 15 years, 30 years, or 100 years?

Q483. In 1896, which was the first African country to defeat a European invasion: South Africa, Nigeria, or Ethiopia?

Indian weapon

Q492. What is one of these called?

Q493. Which Italian national hero fought for his country's unification, and in wars in South America?

Cuisse

Q494. Which light thrusting swords were developed for fencing?

Greave

Q495. For which sport did a knight wear tilting armor?

Q484. After which part of which animal is the above weapon named?

Q485. What happens if you throw a boomerang and miss your target?

Kenyan knife

Q486. Who led the Mongols from obscurity into one of the greatest empires ever?

Sabaton

Q496. On which part of the body was the deadly weapon above worn by the Suks of Kenya?

Clothing

Q497. What did a Viking make with a hand spindle?

Q498. Which French king in the 17th century began a trend for wearing wigs?

Hand spindle and bone threadpickers

Q499. What are made from denim, most often blue, and worn around the world?

Buckle plate

Q500. What did this buckle plate fasten: a belt, a cloak, or a dress?

Q501. Folding fans arrived in Europe in the 16th century. Where did they originate: China, Turkey, or Russia?

Detachable cuffs

Q502. In which century was it fashionable to wear the detachable cuffs above: the 10th, 18th, or 20th century?

Q503. When the first versions of the handbag appeared in the 18th century, did they belong to men or to women?

Gentleman's pouch bag

Q504. When did the miniskirt make its first appearance?

Woman in silk bustle dress

Q505. What is the main use for a fan?

18th-century fan

Q506. In ancient Rome, which garment indicated Roman citizenship?

Q507. In the Middle Ages, were rolls, coils, steeples, butterflies, and horns headdresses, petticoats, or jewels?

Q508. What did wealthy men and women do with these beauty patches?

18th-century beauty patches

Q509. When was this straw hat fashionable: in the early 20th century or the late 18th century?

Straw hat

Roman hairpin

Q510. Why did Roman imperial women need hairpins?

Q511. In the 1500s, it was very fashionable for men to look overweight. Where did this craze originate: Norway, Italy, or Spain?

Q512. The lady to the left is wearing a silk bustle dress from the 1880s. What is a bustle?

Q513. What were chopines: shoes, buckles, or cuffs?

Gentleman's embroidered waistcoat

Q514. When was this waistcoat fashionable: in the 14th, 18th, or 20th century?

Q515. Which material, originally Chinese, was prized in the Byzantine Empire?

Gentleman in 18th-century suit

Accessories

Q On what part of the body would you wear these items?

525.
526.
527.
528.
529.
530.
531.
532.

Hand-embroidered gloves

Q521. In the 1800s, why did upper-class European women keep their hands covered?

Wide ties

Q522. Were wide ties fashionable in the 1770s, 1870s, or 1970s?

Q516. Who were the first people to cut and fit garments, rather than just draping themselves in fabric: the Persians, the Elizabethans, or the Romans?

Q517. Can you name the stiff whalebone petticoat first worn by women in the 1850s to support their skirts?

Q518. Which country influenced fashions throughout Europe for most of the 18th century: Spain, France, or England?

Q519. Since the 1940s, nylon has been used for clothing. What is nylon?

Q520. Was a pompadour a hairstyle or a parasol?

Seamed nylon stockings

Q523. What happened to skirts in Europe and the United States in the 1920s that some people found very shocking?

Q524. In the 1970s, did men wear platform shoes?

1970s platform shoes

Inventions: to 1850

If human beings didn't have a gift for invention and scientific discovery, we would all still live in caves. Homes, clothes, jobs, schools, transportation: every part of modern life depends on the creations of science and invention. We are so surrounded by them that it's hard to imagine life without them.

Model of 17th-century clock made by Dutch mathematician and astronomer Christiaan Huygens

An early electric telegraph

Q 539. Was the earliest electric telegraph made in Europe or the United States?

Q 533. In what did people first take to the air in 1783?

Q 538. In 1802 Zachaus Winzler cooked with a substance never before used for cooking. What was it?

Q 540. Which were built first, baths or showers?

Q 534. In 1656 this feature revolutionized clocks. What is it?

Bifocal eyeglasses

Q 541. Was printing invented in Germany, China, or Japan?

Q 535. Which were constructed earlier, arches or tunnels?

Q 542. Were eyeglasses first peered through in 300, 1300, or 1800?

Q 536. Which was standardized first, the imperial or the metric system of measurement?

Q 537. In 1530 a French invention changed the way that wine was stored and made champagne possible. What was it?

Q 543. Which was invented first, the violin or the piano?

Q 544. Was wallpaper first produced in England, France, or India?

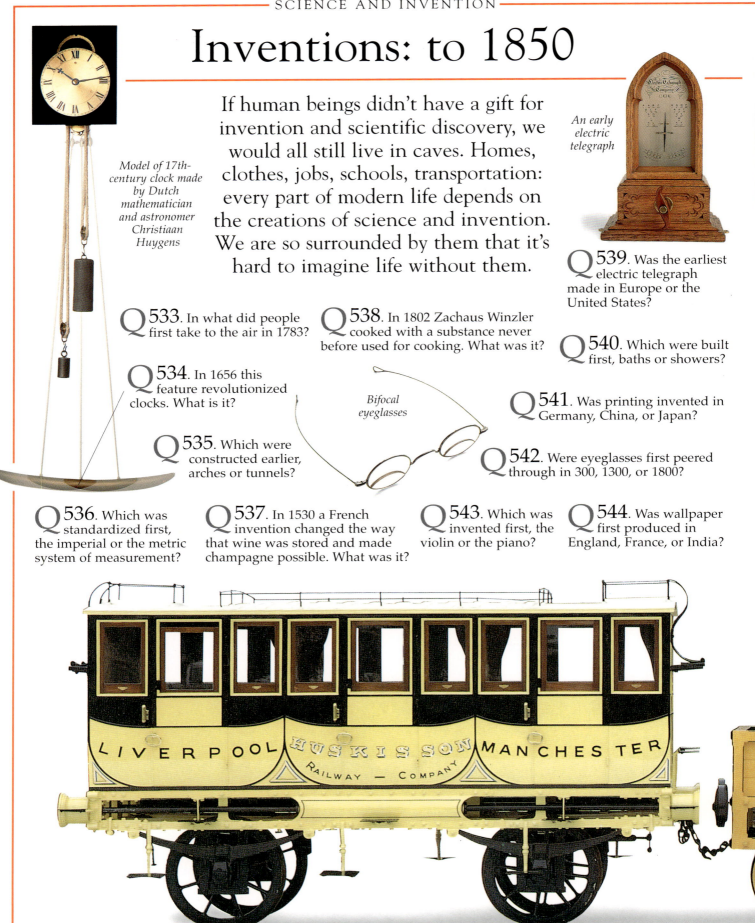

LIVERPOOL HUSKISSON MANCHESTER
RAILWAY — COMPANY

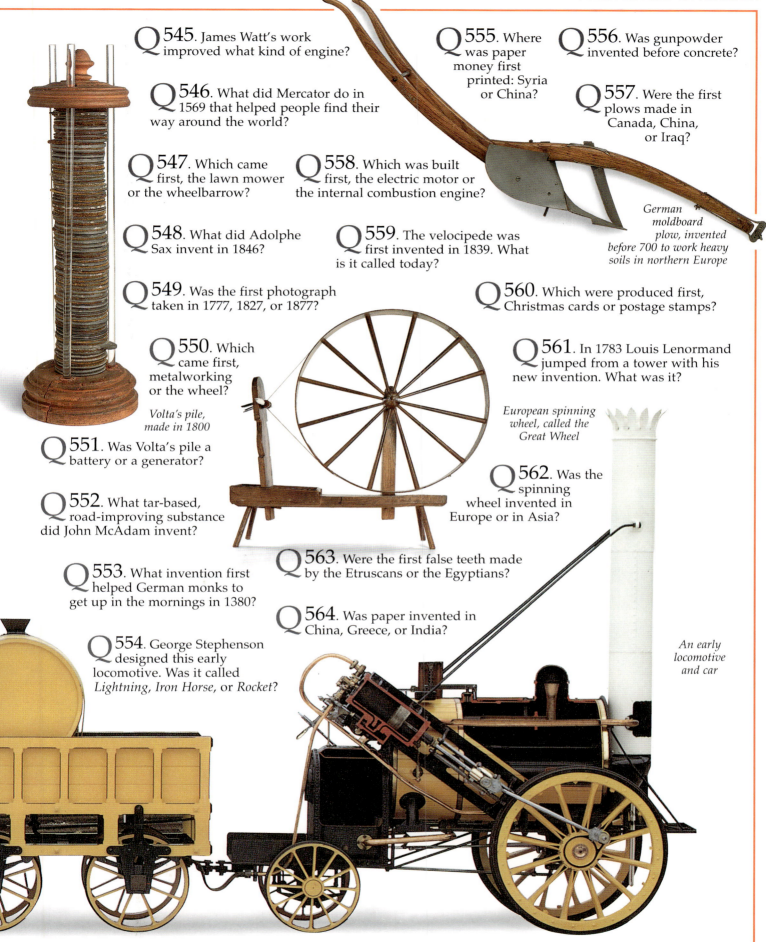

Q545. James Watt's work improved what kind of engine?

Q546. What did Mercator do in 1569 that helped people find their way around the world?

Q547. Which came first, the lawn mower or the wheelbarrow?

Q548. What did Adolphe Sax invent in 1846?

Q549. Was the first photograph taken in 1777, 1827, or 1877?

Q550. Which came first, metalworking or the wheel?

Volta's pile, made in 1800

Q551. Was Volta's pile a battery or a generator?

Q552. What tar-based, road-improving substance did John McAdam invent?

Q553. What invention first helped German monks to get up in the mornings in 1380?

Q554. George Stephenson designed this early locomotive. Was it called *Lightning, Iron Horse,* or *Rocket*?

Q555. Where was paper money first printed: Syria or China?

Q556. Was gunpowder invented before concrete?

Q557. Were the first plows made in Canada, China, or Iraq?

German moldboard plow, invented before 700 to work heavy soils in northern Europe

Q558. Which was built first, the electric motor or the internal combustion engine?

Q559. The velocipede was first invented in 1839. What is it called today?

Q560. Which were produced first, Christmas cards or postage stamps?

Q561. In 1783 Louis Lenormand jumped from a tower with his new invention. What was it?

European spinning wheel, called the Great Wheel

Q562. Was the spinning wheel invented in Europe or in Asia?

Q563. Were the first false teeth made by the Etruscans or the Egyptians?

Q564. Was paper invented in China, Greece, or India?

An early locomotive and car

The Earth

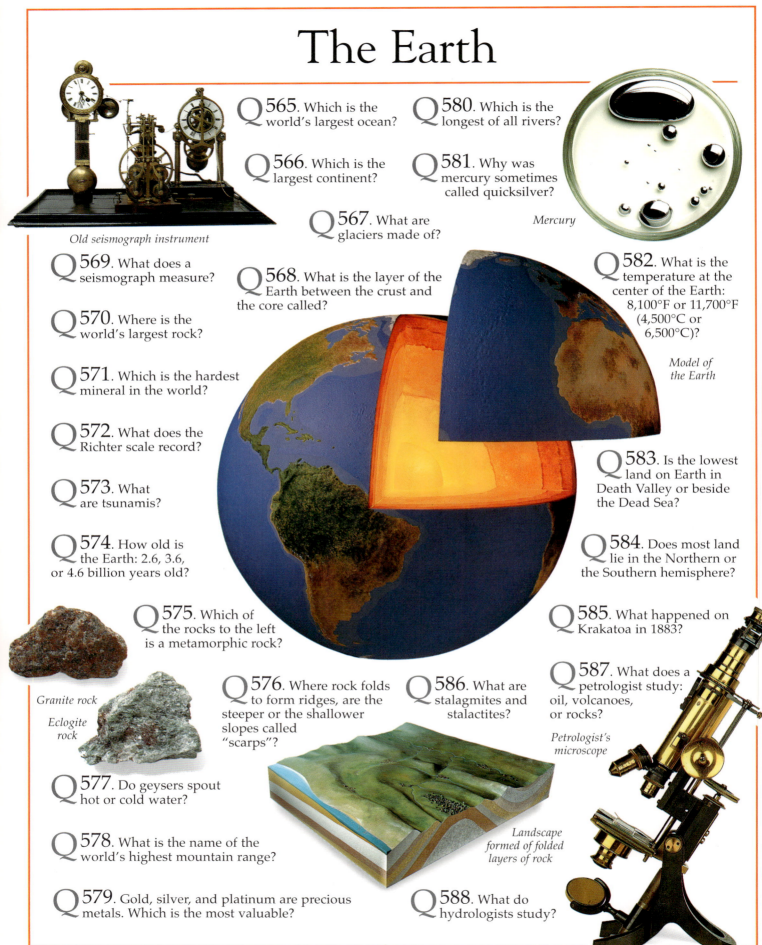

Old seismograph instrument

Mercury

Q **565**. Which is the world's largest ocean?

Q **566**. Which is the largest continent?

Q **567**. What are glaciers made of?

Q **568**. What is the layer of the Earth between the crust and the core called?

Q **569**. What does a seismograph measure?

Q **570**. Where is the world's largest rock?

Q **571**. Which is the hardest mineral in the world?

Q **572**. What does the Richter scale record?

Q **573**. What are tsunamis?

Q **574**. How old is the Earth: 2.6, 3.6, or 4.6 billion years old?

Q **575**. Which of the rocks to the left is a metamorphic rock?

Q **576**. Where rock folds to form ridges, are the steeper or the shallower slopes called "scarps"?

Q **577**. Do geysers spout hot or cold water?

Q **578**. What is the name of the world's highest mountain range?

Q **579**. Gold, silver, and platinum are precious metals. Which is the most valuable?

Q **580**. Which is the longest of all rivers?

Q **581**. Why was mercury sometimes called quicksilver?

Q **582**. What is the temperature at the center of the Earth: 8,100°F or 11,700°F (4,500°C or 6,500°C)?

Model of the Earth

Q **583**. Is the lowest land on Earth in Death Valley or beside the Dead Sea?

Q **584**. Does most land lie in the Northern or the Southern hemisphere?

Q **585**. What happened on Krakatoa in 1883?

Q **586**. What are stalagmites and stalactites?

Q **587**. What does a petrologist study: oil, volcanoes, or rocks?

Petrologist's microscope

Q **588**. What do hydrologists study?

Granite rock

Eclogite rock

Landscape formed of folded layers of rock

Astronomy

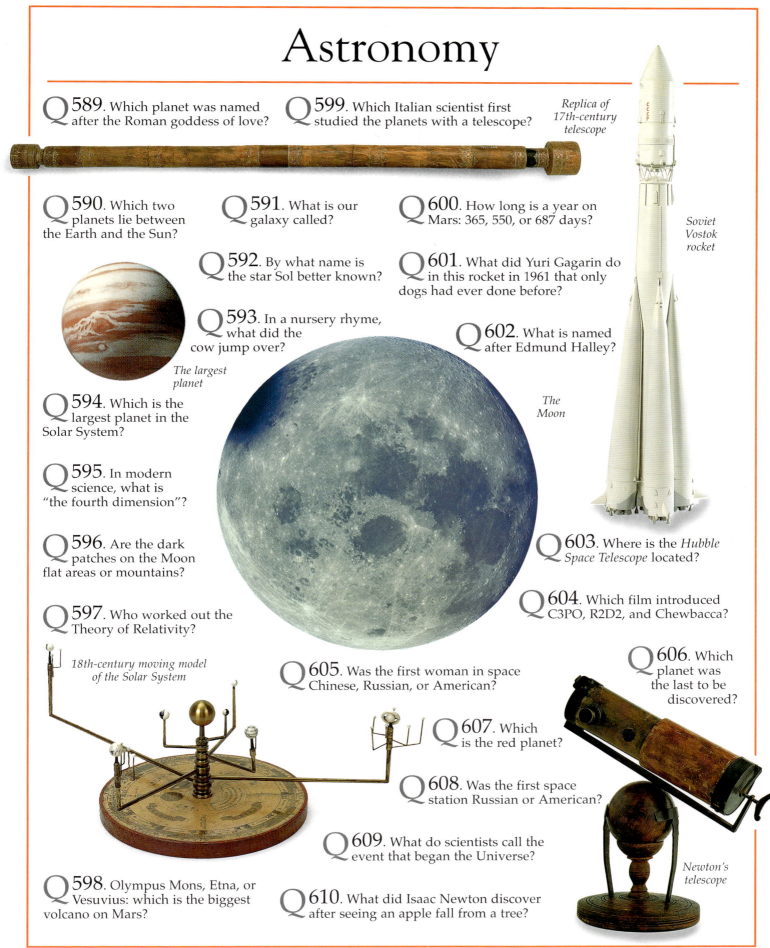

Q589. Which planet was named after the Roman goddess of love?

Q599. Which Italian scientist first studied the planets with a telescope?

Replica of 17th-century telescope

Q590. Which two planets lie between the Earth and the Sun?

Q591. What is our galaxy called?

Q600. How long is a year on Mars: 365, 550, or 687 days?

Soviet Vostok rocket

Q592. By what name is the star Sol better known?

Q601. What did Yuri Gagarin do in this rocket in 1961 that only dogs had ever done before?

Q593. In a nursery rhyme, what did the cow jump over?

The largest planet

Q602. What is named after Edmund Halley?

Q594. Which is the largest planet in the Solar System?

The Moon

Q595. In modern science, what is "the fourth dimension"?

Q596. Are the dark patches on the Moon flat areas or mountains?

Q603. Where is the *Hubble Space Telescope* located?

Q597. Who worked out the Theory of Relativity?

Q604. Which film introduced C3PO, R2D2, and Chewbacca?

Q606. Which planet was the last to be discovered?

18th-century moving model of the Solar System

Q605. Was the first woman in space Chinese, Russian, or American?

Q607. Which is the red planet?

Q608. Was the first space station Russian or American?

Q609. What do scientists call the event that began the Universe?

Newton's telescope

Q598. Olympus Mons, Etna, or Vesuvius: which is the biggest volcano on Mars?

Q610. What did Isaac Newton discover after seeing an apple fall from a tree?

The Human Body

Q611. How many times does a heart beat every day: 100,000, 500,000, or 1,000,000 times?

Q612. Who has more bones: a child or an adult?

Q613. What is the hardest substance in the human body?

Components of the chest

Q614. How many pints of air can a pair of lungs hold: 5, 18, or 26 (3, 10, or 15 liters)?

Q615. Which country has more hospitals than any other?

Q616. Can you name the horny substance in nails, hair, and skin?

Q617. Can you name the female organ in which a baby develops?

Q618. Which is the largest organ of the human body?

Q619. Which doctor founded psychoanalysis, a treatment for mental illness?

Q620. Can you name the bony cage that protects the chest organs?

Q621. In how many directions can the knee joint bend?

Leg and foot bones

Q622. Which intestine is longer: the small intestine or the large intestine?

Q623. About how many muscles are there in the human body: 200, 400, or more than 600?

Tropical papayas

Q624. The tropical fruit papaya can be used to treat threadworms and ringworms. True or false?

Q625. In what year were X rays discovered by Wilhelm Roentgen: 1800, 1850, or 1895?

Thoracic vertebra

Q626. In which part of the human body would you find this bone?

Q627. How heavy is the human head: 4.4 lb, 8.8 lb, or 17.6 lb (2 kg, 4 kg, or 8 kg)?

Medicine chest

Q628. In which century were the medicines above used: the 17th, 18th, or 19th?

Q629. Are fish, eggs, and meat made up of carbohydrates or proteins?

Q630. Which part of the human body does a doctor examine with a gastroscope: the stomach, heart, or lungs?

Q631. Which is the longest bone in the human body: the femur, tibia, or humerus?

Inside the head and neck

Q632. Which French scientist developed vaccines and invented pasteurization (heating to destroy bacteria)?

Q633. How many bones are there in the human body: 106, 206, or 306?

Q634. Which Polish-born French woman discovered the chemical element radium and was awarded the Nobel Prize for chemistry in 1911?

Q635. What is the difference between a local anesthetic and a general anesthetic?

Q636. Who discovered penicillin?

Q637. What is the function of arteries?

Q638. Why did doctors apply bloodsucking leeches to their patients?

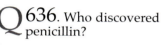

Leeches

Q639. When did the first woman graduate from medical school in the United States: 1810, 1849, or 1934?

Q640. Before 1600 in England why did human dissection take place in secret?

Q641. What did a doctor do with the saw above at the Battle of Waterloo?

Q642. Can you name 2 of the major blood groups?

Saw and glove

Q643. How many muscles does the average adult use when going for a walk: 50, 100, or more than 200?

Q644. Which ancient form of Chinese medicine involves the insertion of needles into various points of the body to treat illnesses?

Q645. Which year was the first test tube baby born: 1978, 1986, or 1990?

Q646. Where is the smallest bone in the human body: in the ear, the foot, or the wrist?

Q647. When was the first successful heart transplant performed: 1937, 1967, or 1987?

Q648. When did dentistry become a recognized profession: in the 15th, 17th, or 19th century?

Q649. Which fluid secreted by the liver aids digestion?

Q650. What does a midwife do?

Q651. Which instrument does a doctor use to listen to the heart and lungs?

Q652. Which year was a syringe first used to inject drugs directly into the body: 1753, 1853, or 1953?

Human skeleton

Hypodermic syringe

Q653. How many bones are there in the hand: 12, 20, or 27?

Q654. In which year was the World Health Organization (WHO) set up by the United Nations: 1908, 1928, or 1948?

Q655. Can you name the bone to which the ribs are attached?

Q656. Can you name 2 of the 5 main senses of the human body?

Q657. Why do people get goose bumps?

Q658. When were anesthetics introduced: in the 1840s, 1880s, or 1920s?

Ether inhaler

Biology and Chemistry

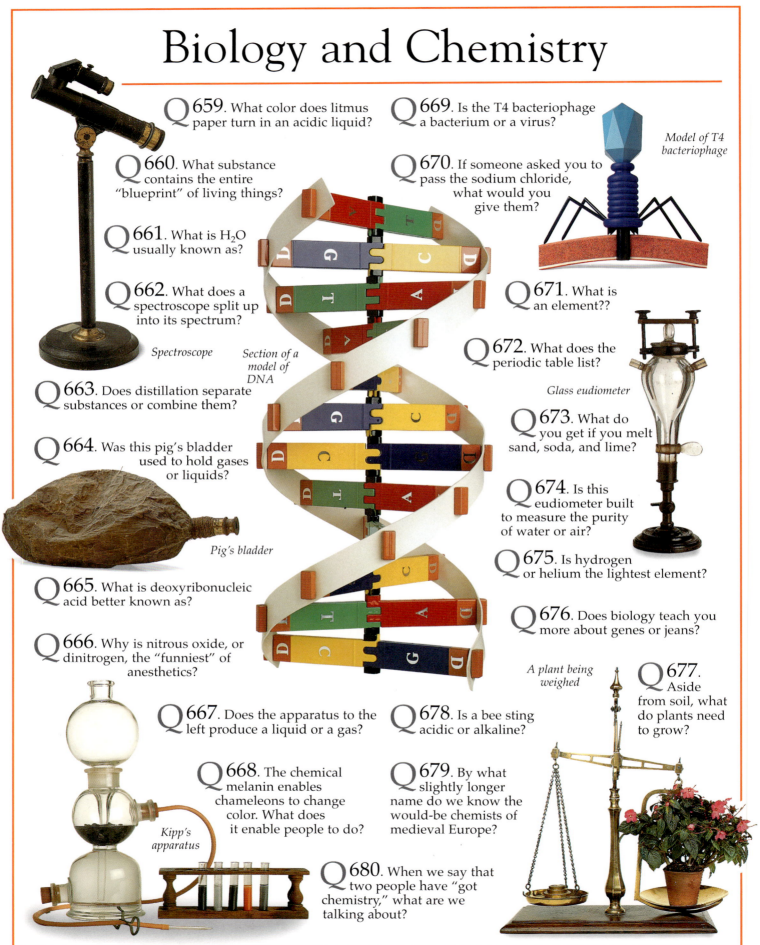

Q659. What color does litmus paper turn in an acidic liquid?

Q660. What substance contains the entire "blueprint" of living things?

Q661. What is H_2O usually known as?

Q662. What does a spectroscope split up into its spectrum?

Spectroscope

Section of a model of DNA

Q663. Does distillation separate substances or combine them?

Q664. Was this pig's bladder used to hold gases or liquids?

Pig's bladder

Q665. What is deoxyribonucleic acid better known as?

Q666. Why is nitrous oxide, or dinitrogen, the "funniest" of anesthetics?

Q667. Does the apparatus to the left produce a liquid or a gas?

Q668. The chemical melanin enables chameleons to change color. What does it enable people to do?

Kipp's apparatus

Q669. Is the T4 bacteriophage a bacterium or a virus?

Model of T4 bacteriophage

Q670. If someone asked you to pass the sodium chloride, what would you give them?

Q671. What is an element??

Q672. What does the periodic table list?

Glass eudiometer

Q673. What do you get if you melt sand, soda, and lime?

Q674. Is this eudiometer built to measure the purity of water or air?

Q675. Is hydrogen or helium the lightest element?

Q676. Does biology teach you more about genes or jeans?

A plant being weighed

Q677. Aside from soil, what do plants need to grow?

Q678. Is a bee sting acidic or alkaline?

Q679. By what slightly longer name do we know the would-be chemists of medieval Europe?

Q680. When we say that two people have "got chemistry," what are we talking about?

Weather and Climate

Q681. In weather terms, what does "cumulus" refer to?

Q682. Is Antarctica, Asia, or Africa the driest continent?

Statue of sun god

Q683. Is this statue Aztec or Egyptian?

Q684. Is high or low pressure a sign of rain?

Q685. What do barometers measure?

Q686. Does the greenhouse effect warm us up or cool us down?

Q687. What is measured by an anemometer?

Barometer

Q688. Does air contain more oxygen or nitrogen?

Q689. What kind of magical arc is formed by rain and bright sunshine?

Q690. Where is the coldest place in the world?

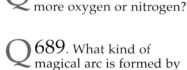

Q691. Does the barograph to the left use an aneroid barometer or a mercury barometer?

Barograph

Q692. Why is San Francisco's Golden Gate Bridge often wrapped in mist?

Q693. What are the northern lights?

Q694. Is the wind at its fiercest or lightest in the eye of a hurricane?

19th-century spinning cup anemometer

Q695. What does a sundial measure?

Sundial

Q696. Is the stratosphere or the troposphere the lowest layer of the atmosphere?

Q697. Where is the mountain that sees rain on 350 days a year?

Q698. In what do "CFCs" (chlorofluorocarbons) create a hole?

Model of weather across a mountain range

Q699. On which side of a mountain range does more rain fall: the side the clouds come from, or the opposite side?

Q700. In thunderstorms, do you hear thunder before you see lightning?

Q701. How do differences in pressure affect the atmosphere?

Model showing how winds circulate

Q702. What causes the Coriolis effect?

Q703. Does hot air rise or fall?

Q704. Are cirrus clouds found at higher altitudes than stratus clouds?

Q705. Is the hottest place in the world in Africa or North America?

Inventions: 1850-1950

Long-playing record, 1948

Q706. What did the Wright brothers do in 1903 that no one had ever done before: fly an airplane, split the atom, or watch TV?

Q707. Which was invented first, the telephone or the fax machine?

"Box telephone"

Q714. Where did the world's first motorway, the Avus Autobahn, open in 1921: Germany, France, or the United States?

Q715. Electric toasters existed at the end of the 19th century, but when was the pop-up toaster invented: in about 1920, 1930, or 1940?

Q708. How long did the first LP (long-playing record) play on each side: 23 minutes, 33 minutes, or 53 minutes?

Hair dryer

Q716. Emilé Berliner created the forerunner of modern records (disks). What did he invent so he could listen to them?

Q709. In which year was the first handheld hair dryer introduced in the United States: 1850, 1870, or 1920?

Q710. What does the car owe to the French Michelin brothers André and Edouard?

Q717. The first motorbike had a wooden frame and wooden wheels. Was it made in 1865, in 1885, or in 1905?

Q711. Which invention, fitted to motor taxicabs in 1896, stopped passengers from arguing with their drivers when they reached their destination?

Q712. Which was the first car to be built on a moving assembly line: the Model T Ford or the Benz Velo?

Q718. Which was invented first, the jet airplane or the helicopter?

First automatic photocopier

Q713. Was the first car built in Germany, the United States, or France?

Q719. In which year did Chester Carlson invent the photocopier: 1859, 1903, or 1938?

An early car

Q720. Which was invented first, the airship, the airplane, or the glider?

An early model airplane

Q729. When was chewing gum first sold: 1852, 1872, or 1942?

Q721. In which city did the first underground railroad open in 1863: London, New York, or Paris?

Q722. ENIAC, built in the United States in 1946, was the first programmable, general-purpose, automatic, electronic computer. Did it weigh 5 tons or 30 tons?

Q730. In what year was the microwave oven invented: 1916, 1926, or 1946?

Q731. Which Italian engineer developed the first radio while experimenting in his parents' attic: Guglielmo Marconi, Samuel Morse, or Roland Moreno?

Q723. When did the first major radio station begin broadcasting: in 1900, 1920, or 1940?

Regina hexaphone jukebox

Q732. When was toilet paper invented: 1857, 1897, or 1937?

Screw-in lightbulb

Q724. In 1914 the first set of traffic signals was installed, in Cleveland, Ohio. How many colors did it show?

Q733. How many tunes did the first jukebox play: 1, 16, or 26?

Q734. Which soft drink launched by American pharmacist John Pemberton has become the world's best-selling drink?

Q725. Thomas Edison patented hundreds of inventions, including the lightbulb. Was he American, English, or French?

Q737. In 1877 Thomas Edison invented the phonograph. What did it do?

Q726. What did James Ritty invent in 1879 to help shop-keepers with their calculations?

Headphones

Q735. What would you have done with this pair of headphones in the 1920s?

Q738. In which year was the first credit card issued: 1920, 1935, or 1950?

Q727. When was the first, black and white television invented: 1903, 1913, or 1926?

Q736. Was the world's first nuclear reactor built on a football field, an ice rink, or a squash court?

Q739. What did the Biro brothers invent in 1938?

Early iron

Q728. The iron was the first electrical device used in the home. True or false?

Zipper

Q740. When did the zipper go on sale: 1829, 1878, or 1914?

Q741. Invented in 1913, it revolutionized food storage. What was it?

The Modern World

Q**742**. What comes out of a black hole?

Q**743**. What can high-tech tinned food now do?

Satellite television dish

Q**744**. What is a PC?

Q**745**. Apart from satellites what other new means of transmitting TV programs is very popular?

Q**746**. How many telephone subscribers were there in the world at the end of 1991: 537 million or 1,537 million?

Q**747**. Which came first, microchips or videotape?

Q**748**. What busily buzzing aid to tooth care was first seen in 1961?

Q**749**. Does superconductivity work at high or low temperatures?

Q**750**. What travels down optical fibers?

Q**751**. What does a smart bomb follow?

Q**752**. What is a Walkman?

Personal computer

Q**753**. Which part of the body does a pacemaker assist?

Q**754**. Was the first artificial heart implanted in 1962 or 1982?

Q**755**. What kind of disk would you insert here?

Q**756**. Which were made first, 3-dimensional holograms or personal computers?

Q**757**. What is one of these called?

Q**758**. Can the world's most powerful microscope magnify objects 1 million times, 100 million times, or 10 billion times?

Q**759**. What makes Harriers different from ordinary aircraft?

Pacemaker

Q**760**. What is the circuit board to the left a part of?

Q**761**. Were the first home video games made in the 1960s or 1970s?

Credit cards

Q**762**. What is a fax?

Q**763**. What is a smart card?

Q**764**. Which country produces the most domestic waste per person: Japan or the United States?

Q**765**. In 1971, which French invention did more than just mix food?

Microchips on a circuit board

Q**766**. What do you do to an icon with a mouse?

Scientific instruments

Q What are the names of the objects below, all of which are used in scientific experiments?

786.

787.

788.

789.

790.

791.

Nuclear fuel rods of uranium from a nuclear reactor

Digital thermometer

Q767. What is the difference between nuclear fission and nuclear fusion?

Q768. Which device provided a new way to listen to music in 1963?

Q769. In 1992, could the world's most powerful computer chip process 4 million, 40 million, or 400 million instructions per second?

Q770. Which missiles can turn corners and follow computerized maps to their targets?

Q771. Which came first, the industrial robot or the digital watch?

Q772. Are the most accurate clocks atomic or mechanical?

Q773. How does genetic fingerprinting identify people?

Q774. What first flew on a cushion of air in 1959?

Q775. Was the first space shuttle launched in 1971, in 1976, or in 1981?

Q776. Which passenger plane was the first to move faster than sound?

Space shuttle

Q777. What is this kind of display called?

Q778. Was *Sputnik* a satellite or a boat?

Q779. What does a wind farm produce?

Q780. Which device works through Light Amplification by Stimulated Emission of Radiation?

2 CDs

Q781. What does CD stand for?

Q782. What game did Erno Rubik invent?

Q783. What do catalytic converters do?

Q784. What is a modem?

Q785. What kind of machines are CD-ROMs designed for?

Soccer

More people play soccer than any other team sport, and professional soccer is the most popular spectator sport in the world. Soccer encourages friendship, discipline, and the ability to work with others. Sponsorship and television are major influences on soccer and leisure activities. Many soccer and sports personalities become millionaires, and sports and leisure events attract huge international audiences.

Lightweight pads

Controlling the ball with the thigh

Q795. On which part of the body must you wear these pads?

Q792. How long does a soccer match last: 60, 90, or 120 minutes?

Q793. In which country was the 1986 World Cup held: Mexico, Spain, or Italy?

Q794. What is the longest time that anyone has juggled a soccer ball in the air without using their hands: 7, 12, or 17 hours?

Underarm throw

Q796. Were the first soccer matches played on grass fields or on the streets?

Soccer cleats

Q797. Which South American country has won the World Cup more times than any other country: Bolivia, Brazil, or Argentina?

Q798. How much does the average soccer cleat weigh: 6, 8, or 10 oz (150, 250, or 350 g)?

Q799. How many players are there on a team?

Q800. Who is the only player who can touch the ball with his or her hands?

Q801. Who patrols the edge of the field to assist the referee?

Q802. In soccer, what is a bicycle kick?

Q803. The referee uses a whistle to indicate the start and end of a match. For what else does the referee use the whistle?

Push passing

Q804. Other than the feet, what parts of the body are frequently used to direct the ball?

Q805. What are the 2 occasions when back passes are not allowed?

Q806. Which member of the team wears an armband and why?

Q807. How many different countries play soccer at the international level: 80, 100, or 140?

Q808. How many shots does each team initially get in a penalty shoot-out: 5, 10, or 15?

Q809. Which team won the 1982 World Cup: Spain, Poland, or Italy?

Pre-1945 soccer ball

Q810. Is this early soccer ball made of rubber, plastic, or leather?

Q811. Which Brazilian soccer player is known as the "Black Pearl"?

Red card

Yellow card

Q812. What is a goalkeeper's punt?

Q813. Which country plays Gaelic soccer: Turkey, Ireland, or Norway?

Q814. Which card is a player given when he or she is sent off the field for a serious offense?

Q815. What does FIFA stand for?

Q816. What is the highest score ever recorded in an international soccer match: 9-2, 16-4, or 17-0?

Q817. Who scored 3 goals in the 1966 World Cup Final: Paolo Rossi, Geoff Hurst, or Diego Maradona?

Q818. Which tenor sang *Nessun Dorma* at the 1990 World Cup: Luciano Pavarotti or Placido Domingo?

Q819. In which area can the goalkeeper pick up the ball?

Goalkeepers' gloves

Q820. Why do goalkeepers dampen their gloves before a game?

Q821. Which African team in the 1990 World Cup was famous for its wiggling hip dance?

Goalkeepers' clothing

Indoor Sports

Q822. Which sport follows Queensberry rules: boxing or horse racing?

Q823. In which of these card games is a royal flush a winning hand: bridge or poker?

Q824. Was the world's youngest ever chess champion Bobby Fischer or Garry Kasparov?

Chess pieces

Q825. Which kind of wrestling began in Japan?

Q826. Which sporting birds are the best at finding their way home?

Q827. Which sport features a puck, a goaltender, and a "sin bin"?

A weightlifting bar with weights attached

Q833. Is it easier to lift weights using the "snatch" technique or the "clean and jerk"?

Q834. Are the Toucan Terribles, the Pernod Rams, and the Black Dog Boozers marbles, volleyball, or football teams?

Boxing glove

Q835. Kung Fu, karate, karaoke: which of these is not a martial art?

Q836. Was Muhammad Ali or Rocky Marciano the only world heavyweight boxing champion never to lose a professional fight?

Q837. In snooker, when are you snookered?

Q838. How many basketballs can one person dribble at a time: 4, 6, or 8?

Snooker balls

Two young basketball players

Q828. Which game was "invented" when skittles, or ninepins, was banned in the United States in 1845?

Q829. Which sport involves vaulting, a beam, rings, and several different kinds of bars?

Q830. Were the blades of the first known ice skates made from metal, plastic, or organic materials?

Ice skate

Q831. In which game do knights, bishops, castles, and the queen work together to protect the king?

Q839. Which game ends when someone pockets the 8-ball: polo, snooker, or pool?

Q832. Was the tallest basketball player on record 7 ft 5 in or 8 ft tall (2.25 m or 2.45 m)?

Outdoor Sports

Q840. Which are bigger: soccer, polo, or football fields?

Q841. In which sport can you bowl a maiden over: cricket, bowling, or tennis?

Q842. In 1985, a 17-year-old German became the Wimbledon men's tennis champion. Who was he?

A tennis player serving

Q843. What is a hat-trick?

Q844. In tennis, what is the difference between a ground stroke and a volley?

Q845. Which sport features birdies, eagles, and bogies?

Q846. In the Scottish Highland Games, the throwing competition is called "tossing the caber." Do the contestants throw a log, a steel cable, or a haggis?

Referee's whistle

Q847. In which of these sports does the referee or umpire use a whistle: tennis, boxing, or soccer?

Q848. Which is the odd ball out: a soccer ball, a football, or a basketball?

Protective shoulder pads

Baseball mitt

Q849. In which sport would these shoulder pads be worn?

Q850. What does a baseball field have that any jeweler in the world would envy?

Q851. If we battled from love to deuce, and then to gain the advantage, which game would we be playing?

Q852. Was the oldest person to finish a marathon 78, 88, or 98 years old?

Q853. Of which nation was it said, "they are good at inventing games and losing them"?

Q854. In which sport is it possible to be stumped by the keeper off a leg-spinner?

A cricket ball hits the stumps

Q855. In car racing, which is the fastest: Formula 1, Formula 2, or Formula 3?

Renault race car

The Olympic Games

Q856. The Olympic symbol is a set of interlocking rings. How many are there?

Q857. What do the Olympic interlocking rings represent: continents, different kinds of sports, or the founding nations of the Olympics?

Q858. What kind of medal is awarded for finishing third?

Q859. When the end of a race is so close that the clock cannot tell which contestant finished first, what means is used to decide who has won?

Q860. Who was the first gymnast to record a perfect score of 10 at the Olympics: Olga Korbut or Nadia Comaneci?

A stopwatch, used for timing sporting events

Q861. When high jumpers use the technique called the "Fosbury Flop," do they go over the bar forward or backward?

Q862. Which sport in the Winter Olympics takes place on "the large hill" and "the normal hill"?

Q863. In the 1988 Olympics, Canadian Ben Johnson won the 100 meter race in world record time, but he did not take home the gold medal. Why not?

Sports shoe, with spikes for better grip on running tracks

Q864. Do the Olympics take place every 2 years, every 4 years, or every 6 years?

A gymnast doing a floor exercise

Q870. How many events are there in the decathlon?

Q871. Which event includes pistol shooting, show jumping, fencing, a swim, and a cross-country run?

Q872. Which all-female Olympic sport involves floor exercises with ribbons, balls, hoops, ropes, and Indian clubs?

Q873. Which infamous world leader objected to handing out medals to the most famous athlete at the 1936 Berlin Olympics?

Q865. Which is the longest distance run at the Olympic Games?

Q866. How is a horse used in gymnastics?

Q867. In which country was the site of the ancient Olympic Games: Italy, Greece, or Israel?

Q868. Only 1 person has ever won 7 gold medals at a single Olympic Games. Was the person who won them a skater, a swimmer, or a runner?

Q869. Which are the only team Olympic track and field events?

Target pistol, used in pistol-shooting competitions

Q874. In pistol-shooting competitions, do the competitors stand up or lie down?

Q875. Which can be thrown farther, the shot put or the discus?

A women's shot put, a men's shot put, and a discus

Q **880**. Which skiing event is the fastest: the slalom, the giant slalom, or the downhill?

A skier tackling the slope

Q **881**. Did the film *Chariots of Fire* feature Olympic sprinters, cyclists, or tobogganists?

Q **882**. Was the person who received 35,000 love letters after winning the gold medal a swimmer, a skier, or a skater?

Q **876**. How many people are there in the crews of the biggest rowing boats at the Olympics: 5, 8, or 9?

Q **877**. What is the greatest number of gold medals won by 1 person in their Olympic career: 8, 10, or 12?

Q **878**. Do boxers in the Olympics wear headguards or not?

Q **883**. How long was the longest Olympic career to date: 30 years, 40 years, or 50 years?

Q **879**. Two of the elements of the triple jump are a step (or skip) and a jump. What is the third element?

Q **884**. In show jumping competitions, do the competitors aim for a high or a low score?

Q **885**. The biathlon is made up of two sports. One is cross-country skiing. What is the other?

Q **886**. Which is the fastest of the swimming styles for which there are Olympic events?

Q **887**. How do Olympic swimmers stop the clock at the end of their races?

Q **888**. Which can be thrown farther, the hammer or the javelin?

Q **889**. Which track race is run over solid, sturdy barriers and a water jump: the high hurdles, the marathon, or the steeplechase?

Q **890**. Where do the competitors usually live during the Olympic Games?

Q **891**. Which Olympic symbol is never allowed to go out?

Q **892**. In which sport do the competitors pose with nose clips on their noses?

Q **893**. Who are the best dancers at the Winter Olympics?

Q **894**. Which of these is *not* an Olympic sport: sailing, basketball, tennis, or bodybuilding?

Q **895**. When were the first modern Olympics held: 1846, 1896, or 1926?

Horse and rider approaching a jump

Q **896**. How many nations competed in the 1992 Olympic Games: 109, 139, or 169?

Q **897**. Which city was successful in its bid to host the Olympics in the year 2000: Manchester, Atlanta, or Sydney?

Q **898**. Is dressage a competition for figure skaters, horse riders, skiers, or bodybuilders?

Swimmer poised to dive

Q **899**. Which country won the most gold medals at the 1944 Olympics: Germany, the United States, or Britain?

1.5 k

Criterion

Art and Architecture

Q900. What do architects do?

Q901. What is the difference between artists and artisans?

The Villa Savoye, designed by the Swiss-born Le Corbusier, whose real name was Charles Édouard Jeanneret

Q902. Where on a church might you find onions and saucers?

Q903. Was this concrete and glass house built during the 18th century, the 19th century, or the 20th century?

Q904. A viaduct is a bridge that carries a road or railroad across a valley. What does an aqueduct carry?

Q905. What do painters do with oil?

An Australian opera house, finished in 1973

Q906. This famous opera house sits on the water's edge and resembles a ship with billowing sails. Where is it: Sydney or Perth?

Q907. Medieval churches often have grotesque heads such as this one carved on the outside. Are they called thunderheads or gargoyles?

Devil with batlike ears

Q908. Which artists make statues?

Model of the spire of Notre Dame cathedral in Paris, France

Q909. Are Corinthian, Doric, and Ionic styles of arches, columns, or windows?

"The Scream," by Norwegian artist Edvard Munch

Q910. Is the style of this painting known as Impressionism or Expressionism?

Q911. What color do you get when you mix blue and yellow paint?

Q912. What art form is created by sticking together tiny pieces of glass or stone?

Tubes of red, yellow, and green paint

Q913. When artists say that they are going to a life class, what are they doing?

Q914. Many bricks are made by baking a soft, squishy material at a high temperature. What is this material called?

Q915. Is it true that Norman arches are pointed and Gothic arches are rounded?

Q916. What is the name given to the very tall buildings first erected in the United States in the late 19th century?

Q917. Out of which material are the best brushes made: sable or horsehair?

Bristle brushes

Dance

Q918. When did ballerinas first dance on pointe (on tiptoe): in the 18th, 19th, or 20th century?

Q919. How many positions of the feet are there in classical ballet: 5, 7, or 10?

Q920. Which elegant and graceful dance originated in Austria in the 18th century?

Q921. Which 1980 US film was set in a school for the performing arts?

Q922. Which ballet dancer starred in the 1948 musical *The Red Shoes:* Moira Shearer, Marilyn Monroe, or Doris Day?

Q923. What did the French gymnast Jules Léotard invent in the 19th century?

Q924. Which legendary dancing duo starred in the 1935 film *Top Hat*?

Jazz dancing

Jazz dancer

Q925. Which 1977 film made John Travolta a disco dancing icon?

Q926. Which strutting, stamping Spanish dance has become famous worldwide?

Q927. Which dance style developed in the streets of New York in the 1980s?

Q928. What fills the tips of pointe shoes?

Q929. Which famous fashion dance was popularized by Madonna?

Ballet shoes

Q930. Which Russian ballet dancer had a meringue-based dessert named after her in Australia?

Q931. Which French king started the first ballet school in 1661: Louis XII, Louis XIV, or Louis XVI?

Q932. What do you call the short, stiff skirt worn by a ballerina?

Q933. Which American actor sang and danced in the rain in 1956?

Q934. Which modern musical is famous for the dancers' daredevil acrobatics on roller skates?

Square dancing

Q935. Who is the person who composes the steps for a ballet or dance?

Q936. Where did square dancing originate: North America, Africa, or Europe?

Music

Baritone

Q937. What do an alto, baritone, wind synth, and tenor have in common?

Q938. Which Italian composer wrote the opera *Aida* in 1871: Antonio Vivaldi, Giuseppe Verdi, Georges Bizet or Richard Wagner?

Q939. Which singer received a platinum record in 1960 to commemorate the sale of his 200 millionth record: Bing Crosby, Frank Sinatra, or Tom Jones?

Q940. Which is the biggest of these stringed instruments: a cello, a guitar, a violin, or a double bass?

Q941. What do Maria Callas, Kiri Te Kanawa, and Luciano Pavarotti have in common?

Q942. What do *The Marriage of Figaro, Don Giovanni*, and *The Magic Flute* have in common?

Guitar

Concert grand piano

Q943. Who uses a baton as a tool?

French horn

Q944. Of which family of instruments are the horn, trombone, and trumpet members: brass, wind, or string?

Q945. Which American rock and roll singer sold millions of records, starred in 33 films, and since his death has become a legend?

Q946. Which piece of classical music composed by George Frederick Handel in 1741 sets parts of the Bible to music?

Q947. What was the popular music of the 17th and early 18th century that was named after the elaborate architectural style of the day: Romanesque, Baroque, or Gothic?

Q948. Who wrote many well-known ballets including *Romeo and Juliet, Swan Lake*, and *Sleeping Beauty*?

Q949. When was the first opera composed: 1297, 1597, or 1897?

Q950. Which 2 members of the Beatles wrote most of the songs?

Q951. How many keys are there on a grand piano: 44, 66, or 88?

20th-century Indian instrument

Q952. Which of the following is an American folk singer most famous for his protest songs of the 1960s: Bob Dylan, Miles Davis, or Jimi Hendrix?

Q953. Who revolutionized jazz in the 1920s with his brilliant solo trumpet playing?

String quartet

Q959. This group of musicians is called a string quartet. Can you identify the four instruments being played?

Q956. Which large, many-stringed instrument is often associated with angels?

Q957. Which legendary, Jamaican reggae star sang *Buffalo Soldier*, *No Woman No Cry*, and *Exodus*?

Q958. Can you name the Swedish group that won the 1974 Eurovision song contest with the hit *Waterloo*?

Flute from Fiji

Nigerian rattle

Rattle on a stick

Indian rattle drum

Q960. How do you play this unusual flute from Fiji?

Q962. Which instrument consists of jingles set into a circular frame and can be held and played while dancing?

Q964. What do you do to make music from a rattle?

Rattle of steel

Q961. What do you do with a didgeridoo?

Q963. A synthesizer can imitate the sounds of all other instruments. What else can it do?

Synthesizer

Q954. What do you call a large group of musicians that performs classical music?

Q965. Can you name the famous musical that opened in London in 1968 and celebrated the ideals of the 1960s, such as peace, love, and freedom: *Hair*, *Grease*, or *The Phantom of the Opera*?

Q966. Can you name the 1961 musical set in New York that is based on *Romeo and Juliet*?

Q955. What is the name of this popular Indian instrument?

Q967. When did the Beatles separate: in 1950, 1960, or 1970?

Movies, TV, and Theater

A spool of film

Q**972**. Who created Mickey Mouse, Donald Duck, *One Hundred and One Dalmations*, and a "magical land" named after himself in California?

Q**973**. Which country was the first to have a regular TV broadcasting service: the United States, Britain, or France?

Q**979**. What is a film story called?

The storyline of a film

Q**968**. How much film is used in each minute of a movie: 23 ft, 90 ft, or 155 ft (7 m, 27 m, or 47 m)?

Q**969**. How many Olympic swimming champions have gone on to play the role of Tarzan in the movies: 1, 2, or 4?

Technicolor three-strip movie camera of 1932

Q**970**. He wrote *Hamlet*, *King Lear*, and *Twelfth Night*, and many of his plays were first performed at the Globe Theatre. Who was he?

Q**974**. Why was this camera called a "three-strip" camera?

Q**975**. In theater, what is the opposite of comedy?

Q**976**. Which sports event has the greatest television audience: the Olympic Games or the soccer World Cup?

Q**977**. What made the 1927 film *The Jazz Singer* a landmark in movie history?

Q**978**. Where are you likely to find stalls, boxes, a tier, and an upper tier?

Q**980**. In which country did European theater begin: Greece, Britain, or Italy?

Q**981**. Which fictional character has appeared in more films than any other: Dracula or Sherlock Holmes?

Q**982**. What happened in the United States in 1983 to lift up television broadcasting to new heights?

Q**983**. In an animated film, how many pictures are needed for each second of action: 6, 12, or 24?

Materials for animation

Q**971**. What is a couch potato?

The Globe Theatre in Southwark, London, England

A zoopraxiscope; it was rotated as light was projected through it

Movie memories

Q With which films, film stars, or characters are the following objects linked?

Q 984. What was the zoopraxiscope designed to create?

Q 985. Is this device a personal organizer, a traffic monitoring computer, or a TV?

Miniaturized design

Q 986. Which town in California is the most famous center of movie production in the world?

Q 987. Who directed *Jurassic Park*, *E.T.*, and *Jaws*: Steven Spielberg or George Lucas?

Film director's chair

996.

997.

998.

1000.

999.

1001.

Q 988. How many times a second is a TV image renewed: 5, 25, or 50 times?

The inside of a 1930s television set

Q 989. In a film crew, what does a boom operator operate: a tape system or a microphone?

Q 990. In films, when sound engineers are creating special effects, what gruesome sound do they imitate by sawing a cabbage in half?

Q 991. Was this camera made in the United States or France?

Hand-cranked camera used in silent films

Q 992. On a film set, what does the director say to stop the cameras?

Theater ticket

Empire Theatre
MATI
BACK
10d.

re Theatre, Chatham.
ATINEE
STALLS
Tax 2d.

Q 993. In which country are the most films made: the United States, India, or France?

Q 994. In which country do people make the greatest number of trips to the movies in a year: the United States or China?

Q 995. Which is the only film to have won 11 Oscars: *Ben Hur*, *Gone with the Wind*, or *Home Alone*?

Answers

Prehistoric life

1 Yes, a "super-continent" called Pangaea.

2 About 165 million years.

3 Flowers first appeared in the age of the dinosaurs.

4 No, it means "terrible lizard."

5 Three; *Triceratops* means "three-horned face."

6 1842; dinosaurs had been described earlier, in 1824, but the name was not thought up until 1842.

7 *Archaeopteryx*, the only feathered one of the 3.

8 Crocodiles and alligators.

9 65 mya. They disappeared surprisingly suddenly; it is not known why.

10 Turtles are the oldest.

11 It was named after the iguana lizard, in 1825.

12 Amber; sometimes insects are preserved in it.

13 Its tiny brain was the size of a walnut.

14 Spiked lizard; it had spikes on its head.

15 A skin sail; its purpose is not known.

16 Only 5 hen's eggs would make up 1 *Hypselosaurus* egg.

17 The size of a dog.

18 It grew up to 50 ft (15 m) long.

19 Yes, 170 million years before any birds.

20 *Tyrannosaurus*; rex means king.

21 *Jurassic Park*, the highest-earning film of all time.

22 *Pteranodons*; "cousins" of the dinosaurs.

23 On its head; these tiny teeth may have been for hitching rides on other sharks.

24 A plant eater.

25 It was thought to have died out with the dinosaurs. It is a "living fossil."

26 We don't know; colors were not preserved.

27 The spiked thumb was for defense.

28 *Lucy in the Sky with Diamonds* by the Beatles, which was on the radio when she was found.

29 The show is *The Flintstones*.

30 Coal; it has been mined for hundreds of years for use as fuel.

31 Cars cannot move without fuel, which comes from oil, and oil comes from fossils.

32 Woolly mammoths, or the similar mastodons.

33 The Himalayas, which are still growing, slowly.

34 4; "tetra" comes from the Greek word for 4.

35 No; the blue whale is the largest ever.

36 The United States; China ranks second.

37 Yes, and remains of elephants, rhino, and a lion.

Reptiles and Amphibians

38 The saltwater crocodile can be 26 ft (8 m) long.

39 A Marion's tortoise lived more than 152 years.

40 No, but it looks like the poisonous coral snake.

41 Off the coast of Australia. It is a Belcher sea snake.

42 Only 0.7 in (18 mm) long, not counting the tail, it is the British Virgin Island gecko.

43 Some snakes can have up to 400 vertebrae.

44 Temperature; eggs develop faster if warmer.

45 A tortoise; it won a race against a hare.

46 It is an awful-smelling turtle.

47 A lizard; Indonesia's Komodo dragons are the biggest lizards in the world, up to 10.2 ft (3 m) long.

48 It is the size of a basketball.

49 3; the third eye is on the top of its head.

50 They change color to match their surroundings.

51 No, they are cold-blooded.

52 It was a leatherback turtle.

53 Because the ground gets too hot for its feet. It lifts its legs up alternately, as if dancing.

54 Alligators are the missing members.

55 They eat mosquitoes and flies.

56 It is the gaboon viper, found in Africa. Its fangs can be 2 in (50 mm) long.

57 30 minutes, moving at 0.1 mph.

58 A lizard, the six-lined racerunner of the Americas. It has been timed at 18 mph (29 kph).

59 The frog turns into a handsome prince. Unfortunately, in real life this doesn't work.

60 It has special poison glands all over its skin.

61 In water; each egg is surrounded by jelly.

62 Yes; it looks like a worm but has teeth.

63 Frogs; toads usually have dry, warty skin.

64 Because its eyeballs move inward when it blinks and help push the food down.

65 In pouches on each side of its body.

66 It could kill 1,500 people.

67 Kenneth Grahame's *The Wind in the Willows*.

68 In fire, according to legend.

69 A hellbender is a kind of salamander.

70 They are the only amphibians with tails.

71 It can eat as many as 100 in one night.

72 They are 4 weeks old; they become frogs at about 12 weeks.

73 By being brightly colored.

74 Frogmen, who swim underwater.

75 *The Muppet Show*, in which Kermit the frog was loved by Miss Piggy.

76 Goliath; these frogs can be 16 in (40 cm) long.

77 Because most amphibians start their lives in water and later move onto land.

78 Just over 17 ft (5 m) for a single jump.

79 No, those with short legs just walk, crawl, or make short hops.

Life in the Ocean

80 It is an angelfish.

81 The oceans are the largest by far.

82 The narwhal, known as the unicorn of the seas.

83 Bull sharks; they sometimes swim up rivers.

84 Sperm whales; their brains can weigh up to 20.2 lb (9.2 kg).

85 To dig up shellfish from the seabed.

86 The Portuguese man-of-war; it has half a million stingers.

87 No; a shark's skeleton is made of cartilage.

88 Simple animals that filter food from the water.

89 Yes, but they have to wake up every few minutes to surface and breathe.

90 A squid seizes prey with its suckers and then paralyzes it with a deadly nerve poison.

91 The blue-ringed octopus is the deadliest.

92 To confuse their enemies.

93 *Through the Looking-Glass*.

94 Yes, the flying fish has enlarged fins that act as wings, allowing it to glide above the waves.

95 It has a pouch in which babies grow safely.

96 No, it is supported by its shell.

97 Blue whales eat 4 tons of krill a day.

98 They grow a new shell under the old one.

99 A shark is a fish and a dolphin is a mammal.

100 The Philippino dwarf pygmy goby at only 0.3 in (8 mm) long.

101 The razor-toothed piranha of South America; some will attack anything.

102 It uses its arms to force open shellfish, turns its stomach inside out onto the prey, and digests it.

103 The sunfish; one specimen was found carrying 300 million eggs.

104 The orca or killer whale will snatch seals and sea lions on some beaches.

105 It lies on the seabed; its patterned body acts as camouflage.

106 A group of fish swimming together is a school.

107 Because its eggs are eaten as caviar.

108 They are insulated by a thick layer of fat, or blubber, that lies just beneath their skin.

109 They evolved thousands of years ago.

110 It inflates to make itself look as large and ferocious as possible.

111 Pisces; it is the biological group that includes all fish.

112 The archerfish; it can leap out of the water, squirt its prey, and knock it down.

113 The blue clam can live for 100 years.

114 The lungfish, it can breathe air through its lungs.

115 The sperm whale measures up to 66 ft (20 m); a giant squid measures up to 59 ft (18 m).

116 No; sea lions, seals, and walruses are pinnipeds. Dolphins are cetaceans.

117 A great white shark has three rows of teeth.

118 A catfish uses its sensitive whiskers to select food.

119 The swordfish's snout can be 5 ft (1.5 m) long.

120 It stings with its tentacles.

121 The hermit crab will change its borrowed shell for a new one as it grows.

122 It raises spines along its back to sting you.

Dogs and Cats

123 The Tasmanian wolf is a marsupial.

124 False; there are about 400 breeds.

125 Ears back show fear or submission.

126 Pluto is Mickey Mouse's dog.

127 The dingo of Australia is probably the most direct ancestor of domestic dogs.

128 "Dog collar" is slang for a priest's clerical collar.

129 *The Hound of the Baskervilles*.

130 Foxes hunt on their own.

131 The fennec fox, which lives in the Sahara.

132 The prairie dog is a North American rodent.

133 Laika, a Russian dog, in 1957.

134 They walk on their toes.

135 Smell; it uses its nose to hunt and find a mate.

136 Sirius, the Dog Star.

137 Its mane; most dogs have no mane.

138 A female fox is called a vixen.

139 Because they are near-sighted.

140 Romulus and Remus; they founded Rome.

141 The fox cub is 10 weeks old.

142 Up to 386 sq miles (1,000 sq km).

143 16 hours; twice as long as most mammals.

144 He strangled the Nemean lion.

145 The cheetah; it can run 60–63 mph (95–100) kph.

146 The Manx cat has no tail.

147 *The Cat Who Walked by Himself.*

148 The lion has a magnificent mane.

149 To hunt larger animals and protect their young.

150 Lionesses, but the lions always eat first.

151 The cheetah can't retract its claws.

152 T. S. Eliot (*Old Possum's Book of Practical Cats*).

153 Leo is named after the lion.

154 The sand cat, which lives in the Sahara Desert.

155 In London, in 1871.

156 Tigers: male Siberian tigers average 10.3 ft (3.15 m) in length.

157 Black leopards are better known as panthers.

158 The Mochica would have worshiped it.

159 *Puss in Boots* was created by Charles Perrault.

160 The lion in the Narnia stories was named Aslan.

161 The ancient Egyptians believed cats were sacred.

162 Yes, all big cats roar, but they cannot purr.

163 Catnip; when cats smell it, they get excited.

Mammals

164 No, bats have perfectly good eyesight.

165 The result is a mule.

166 To help balance itself when walking along branches high up in treetops.

167 A hedgehog rolls into a ball to protect its belly.

168 The matriarch, responsible for the herd's safety.

169 Yes – it lies on its back and wraps itself in seaweed so it won't be swept away by the current.

170 African elephants are bigger, with longer tusks.

171 A porcupine turns its back on its foe, rattles its quills, grunts, and then reverses into its enemy.

172 A hard substance called ivory.

173 The koala will only eat the leaves of certain eucalyptus trees.

174 It is a warm-blooded animal with fur that gives birth to live babies and feeds its young on milk.

175 Chimpanzees make their own tools.

176 To protect their hoofs from damage.

177 Over 6 months in cold climates.

178 They graze in groups; their stripes make it hard for lions to pick out an individual from the herd.

179 To keep themselves cool in hot weather.

180 Sea cows, which graze on sea plants.

181 22 months, longer than any other animal.

182 An animal with a pouch in which to carry babies.

183 Only the platypus and the echidna lay eggs.

184 In the mountains of South America.

185 The mole.

186 Every 4 weeks.

187 Herbivores only eat plants.

188 Moby Dick was white.

189 Apes are more closely related.

190 Giant pandas eat mainly bamboo; large areas of bamboo forest in China have been cut down.

191 Yes; along with apes and humans. Primates have large brains.

192 A rabbit lives in a warren.

193 Kitti's hog-nosed bat; it weighs 0.5 oz (1.5 g).

194 For social reasons, as well as for fur care.

195 Hamsters "carry" food in cheek pouches.

196 Walking, trotting, cantering, and galloping.

197 True, their wings are really webbed hands.

198 In hands; a hand equals 4 in (10 cm).

199 A baby hare is a leveret.

200 It sprays a horrible smelling liquid at enemies.

201 A sloth; it moves very slowly and only wakes up at night.

202 Zaire (but estimates of elephant numbers vary).

203 Run at each other and clash heads and horns.

204 A male moose may weigh 1,000 lb (450 kg).

205 All bears can swim and are happy in water.

206 Beavers build dams to stop flowing water.

207 A weasel grows a white coat in snowy winters.

Birds and Mini-beasts

208 The ostrich, the world's largest bird.

209 The tundra swan; it has over 25,000 feathers.

210 The peacock; the "eyes" are blue patches.

211 To help determine the sounds of their prey.

212 In his belly feathers, which act like a sponge.

213 Snakes; its long legs have tough scales to protect it against poisonous snakebites.

214 Above; this reduces the air pressure above the wing, which creates an upward lift.

215 90 beats per second have been recorded for the horned sungem, a South American hummingbird.

216 7 miles (11 km); one Ruppell's vulture hit an aircraft at that height.

217 Saliva; they make little cup-shaped nests of it.

218 The peregrine falcon; it has been timed in dives at up to 217 mph (350 kph).

219 The sooty tern stays in the air for 3–10 years after leaving its nesting grounds.

220 The Arctic tern, which migrates between the Arctic summer and the Antarctic summer (the longest migration of any bird).

221 The white dove is a symbol of peace.

222 A robin's heart beats 600 times a minute.

223 The Australian pelican; it has a bill up to 18.5 in (47 cm) long.

224 The bee hummingbird of the Caribbean.

225 Icarus; the wax on his wings melted when he flew too close to the sun.

226 The male emperor penguin.

227 None; the last one died in a zoo in 1914.

228 Hollow; but many flightless and diving birds have solid bones.

229 An albatross; the wingspan of the wandering albatross can reach 12 ft (3.6 m).

230 It is the only bird with a sideways-curving bill.

231 The bee is their model.

232 4 pairs of shoes; it has 8 legs.

233 Bombardier beetles fire a gas from their rear ends, with a pop. It forms a smoke screen.

234 It is called the giraffe weevil.

235 In Brazil; it is called the wandering spider.

236 They are female; the drones are male.

237 Speed; they can run at over 10 mph (16 kmph).

238 511; charmed by a farmer's son.

239 Silk; the silkworm becomes a large white moth.

240 In tests, it supported 850 times its own weight.

241 It is thought that they navigate by the light of the Moon and the stars.

242 0.02 in (0.4 mm); as big as the head of a pin.

243 Elephant beetles are the largest.

244 Ultraviolet light.

245 They become butterflies or moths.

246 Nephila spiders' webs are used for fishing.

247 To attract a mate.

248 20 ft (6 m) for one orb weaver spider's web.

Flowers and Plants

249 They are called blossoms.

250 The sweet chestnut; horse chestnuts are inedible.

251 The leaves fall off.

252 Cedar trees are coniferous; they have needlelike leaves and cones and keep their leaves all year.

253 A young tree is a sapling.

254 It flowers for 1 growing season, then it dies.

255 Yes, aloe vera and jojoba are 2 of many plants used in cosmetics.

256 The sap of the sugar maple.

257 Tulips grow in abundance in Holland.

258 Oak trees are broad-leaved; their leaves drop off in the fall.

259 No; ferns, mosses, liverworts, and lichens don't.

260 The male part of a flower is the stamen.

261 The maidenhair tree of China.

262 The Aztecs were the first.

263 The stems can store water.

264 A monkey puzzle is a coniferous tree.

265 The process is called photosynthesis.

266 They open in dry weather.

267 The US giant sequoia can stand 275 ft (83 m) tall.

268 You can eat the seeds.

269 Because they are allergic to pollen in the air.

270 The female part of a flower is the carpel.

271 True; it is made up of many tiny flowers.

272 To transport water and minerals.

273 The transfer of pollen from the male part of a flower to the female part.

274 By the seashore.

275 The giant rafflesia; its flowers can be 32 in (80 cm) across.

276 A sugary liquid produced by a flower.

277 The petals fall off and the seed ripens.

278 It is called resin.

279 Chlorophyll, it collects energy from sunlight.

280 Pollen is carried by animals, insects, or wind.

281 A simple leaf has only 1 leaf, a compound leaf has several leaves, called leaflets.

282 By night, to attract night-flying insects.

283 It helps the tree by providing it with nutrients.

284 By its prickly leaves or unpleasant taste.

285 A forest in its natural, untouched state.

286 The oak tree produces acorns.

287 Garlic is supposed to repel vampires.

288 Pan was the Greek god of forests and flocks.

289 Yes, Venus's – flytrap.

290 You count the tree rings on a cut stump.

291 To attract animals and insects for pollination.

292 Ray florets.

293 Disk florets.

294 Pollen.

295 Ray florets.

296 Stem.

Ancient Egypt

297 The embalmed body of a person (or animal).

298 The pharaohs were the kings of Egypt.

299 His eye; the eye of Horus was said to protect everything behind it.

300 It was a collection of spells meant to help a dead person on the voyage to the next world. It was often put in tombs.

301 They used papyrus, made from the papyrus reed that grows along the Nile River.

302 The sphinx, a magical creature with the body of a lion and the head of a king.

303 The west, the side of the sunset.

304 It was seen as a way of cleansing the spirit.

305 A hippopotamus; as women gave birth, they prayed to Taweret to protect them.

306 94 years; Pepy II became pharaoh when he was 6, and was still on the throne when he was 100 – the longest known reign of any monarch.

307 As special tombs for the pharaohs.

308 The Sun god; the Egyptians believed that Khepri, who was a form of the Sun god, rolled the sun across the sky in the same way that the scarab beetle rolls a ball of dung over the ground.

309 Nut; she was the mother of the Sun god.

310 Tutankhamun, whose tomb was discovered intact by Howard Carter in 1922.

311 It was the symbol of life.

312 The cobra goddess. Only kings and queens wore images of the cobra goddess who, it was thought, spat death at their enemies.

313 Cleopatra, subject of plays, books, and films.

314 About 7.2 million tons. It contains over 2.3 million stone blocks.

315 Heh, god of "millions of years."

316 Reed sandals were the most common footwear at all levels of society. Leather was also worn.

317 They were sacred; 4 million mummified ibises have been found in one animal cemetery.

318 The black land, the land along the Nile, named for its rich black soil. The red land was the desert.

319 Mourning; if a pet cat died, a whole household might shave their eyebrows. Cats were sacred.

320 It was a popular board game, in which players made a symbolic journey through the underworld to the kingdom of the god Osiris.

321 From linen; they were usually white.

322 In the Valley of the Kings.

323 It was unlucky. Red reminded Egyptians of the desert and often represented bad fortune.

324 Yes; St. Paul's is 360 ft (110 m) high; the Great Pyramid, built about 2500 BC, is 450 ft (138 m) high. It was once 481 ft (147 m); it has crumbled a little.

325 An ancient Egyptian form of writing; pictures and symbols represent objects, ideas, and sounds.

Ancient Greece

326 For Zeus, king of the gods.

327 Piraeus; the modern Greek name is Piraius.

328 Greek foot soldiers were called hoplites, from the Greek word *hoplon*, meaning "shield."

329 Pegasus, tamed by the hero Bellerophon.

330 A doctor who recommended good diet and exercise.

331 Go shopping: it was the marketplace, and a meeting place.

332 They dedicated them to the god Apollo and the goddess Artemis as a sign that they had reached the end of childhood.

333 Helen of Troy; in legend, she ran away from Greece to Troy and a Greek army sailed to Troy, fought a war and destroyed the city to get her back.

334 A banquet or formal drinking party where Greek men discussed politics and philosophy.

335 Electrum, a mixture of gold and silver.

336 You would find it on top of a column.

337 The minotaur, said to live in the palace of Knossos on the island of Crete.

338 A Greek warship with 3 (tri) rows of oars.

339 Wine was the favorite, enjoyed by everybody.

340 The Parthenon, built from white marble in 447–438 BC to honor the goddess Athena.

341 Homer (8th century BC); the *Iliad* tells the story of the fall of Troy. He also wrote the *Odyssey*.

342 Poseidon; for both he was the god of the sea.

343 Democracy, the system in which all citizens have the chance to vote for their rulers.

Ancient Rome

344 In a hospital; these utensils were used to explore wounds and hold incisions open.

345 He used either a trident or a dagger, but his net was his main weapon.

346 Gladiator fights and animal fights, all paid for by the Roman emperor to gain popularity.

347 At the baths; Romans cleaned themselves by putting oil on their skin, then scraping it off with strigils.

348 5,000 foot soldiers, usually.

349 Yes, floors were raised so that underfloor hot air could warm them.

350 4; chariot races were major events, watched by up to 250,000 people.

351 A Roman emperor; the laurel wreath symbolized success and power.

352 Julius Caesar, who conquered Gaul (France).

353 XVI; a hundred would be C.

354 So their foot soldiers could see them and follow them in battle.

Medieval Life

355 Robin Hood, the famous English outlaw.

356 A horse; this enameled pendant was part of an elegant harness.

357 In a kitchen, to lift pieces of meat in and out of cauldrons of boiling water.

358 A kirtle, worn with a skirtlike surcoat.

359 In the 15th century; before then wool was woven into cloth on a loom.

360 A moat; some contain water, others are dry.

361 Round towers; they were built more and more often instead of square ones.

362 A weapon; it was a kind of mace with its head swung on a chain.

363 The hornpipe; a leather band connects its wooden pipe to its hollowed-out cow's horn.

364 No; a villein was a peasant who was tied to his lord, unable to leave him.

365 France; at the age of 19, she led the French army to victory over English invaders.

366 The right to pasture pigs in a forest.

367 The keep (or donjon) is the central tower.

368 A great plague of the 14th century. It caused black swellings on its victims, most of whom died.

369 Retrievers; poachers sometimes trained pigs to fetch the birds that they had shot.

370 A squire; when he became a knight he was given sword and spurs.

371 A horse's head; called a shaffron, the armor usually consisted of a headpiece, spike, and plume.

372 His gauntlet; "throwing down the gauntlet" has come to refer to any kind of challenge.

373 It was called the curtain wall.

374 The rose. They were called the Wars of the Roses because the Lancastrians (symbol red rose) fought the Yorkists (white rose) for the crown.

375 At Christmas in a carol.

376 Soccer, then violent, with few rules.

377 Christian attempts to conquer Palestine (now Israel).

378 They are different kinds of silk.

379 So that the defenders could drop unpleasant substances, such as quicklime and boiling oil, through the holes onto people attacking the castle.

380 William Tell of Switzerland. He was being punished for resisting invaders. He hit the apple.

381 The slapstick; hence slapstick comedy.

382 The dungeon, called the oubliette because prisoners might be left there and forgotten.

Renaissance

383 A doublet, made of black silk velvet heavily overstitched in gold thread.

384 In Florence, in the 15th century.

385 Rebirth, describing a great revival of art and learning in 15th- and 16th-century Europe.

386 Velvet; slashed sleeves were very popular.

387 Nicholaus Copernicus, who suggested that the planets in the Solar System orbit the Sun.

388 Ancient Greece inspired the Renaissance.

389 The Hapsburgs, Holy Roman emperors, whose power reached a peak with Charles V (1519–56).

390 It demanded reform in the Catholic church.

391 Italian Leonardo da Vinci, an all-around genius.

392 Elizabeth I, who gave her name to her age.

393 The Medici family.

394 *Romeo and Juliet*.

395 The Gutenberg press was invented in Germany.

396 Gutenberg's Bible was written in Latin.

Exploration

397 English Captain James Cook, who made 3 voyages to the Pacific in the 1760s and 1770s.

398 Measured distances on charts.

399 American astronaut Neil Armstrong when he became the first person to walk on the Moon.

400 Seafaring explorers from Scandinavia.

401 They used their knowledge of winds, currents, and the stars to estimate distance and direction.

402 To frighten people who saw them coming.

403 An ancient trade route across Asia, linking China and Europe.

404 Timbuktu is south of the Sahara desert. It was for centuries an important trading city.

405 Measured time and longitude.

406 China; he served its emperor from 1275–1292.

407 Longships; Vikings also used larger, fatter ships called knarrs for travel and trade.

408 He thought he was in Asia, which is why the islands are known as the West Indies.

409 To identify landmarks from great distances.

410 *On the Origin of Species*.

411 A sextant. Invented in 1757, it is used to judge latitude.

412 By a Frenchman, Louis Blériot.

413 Ferdinand Magellan, but he never completed the journey. When he reached the Philippines in 1521, he was killed.

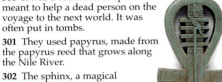

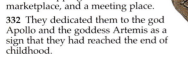

414 Mungo Park was a Scotsman who explored the Niger River in 1795–96 and 1805–06.

415 Christopher Columbus was Italian, but his voyage to the New World was sponsored by King Ferdinand and Queen Isabella of Spain.

416 The American Charles Lindbergh. He flew from New York to Paris in 1927.

417 Yes, he did, with 4 other men, on January 17, 1912. But they all died on the trek back to base camp.

418 Sir Walter Raleigh brought back potatoes and tobacco to Europe. Sir Francis Drake was the first Englishman to sail around the world.

419 Sinbad the Sailor.

Aztecs and Incas

420 Drowning, in wells. Other methods were also used.

421 Silver: the eyes are obsidian and shell, and the mosaic pieces are turquoise and coral.

422 The Aztecs: they believed that the world had ended 4 times, and that the Sun would die a fifth time unless they fed it with human blood.

423 Tlaloc was god of rain.

424 The Aztecs' elite warriors were named the Jaguar Knights and the Eagle Knights.

425 The llama (and other animals in its family).

426 The wheel; the Incas (and the Aztecs) may have used it for toys, but not for transportation.

427 To capture prisoners for sacrifice.

428 All Peruvian men carried them.

429 The Mexica, the Aztecs' name for themselves.

430 In Peru; the Nazca made magnificent textiles.

431 The jaguar, often seen as a symbol of power in ancient Central and South America.

432 Grow crops: chinampas were fertile plots of land built up from swampy parts of Lake Texcoco.

433 Horses; the conquistadors brought horses, guns, and steel weapons, all unknown to the Aztecs. They also introduced the cow to the Americas.

434 They all originated in the Americas.

435 It was surrounded by water. Tenochtitlan was built on a swampy island on a lake; Venice is built on islands in a lagoon.

436 Tenochtitlan, with maybe 200,000 people. The population of London was about 40,000.

The Wild West

437 The Stetson, designed by John B. Stetson, whose hat factory opened in 1865.

438 John Wayne, a famous US actor.

439 They are better known as buffalo.

440 The Peacemaker; it was a Colt .45.

441 Rawhide, which shrank to fit the frame as it dried. It was then covered with finished leather.

442 Europeans called the Dakota nation the Sioux.

443 Custer's: General George Custer led 215 men into an ambush by North American Indians. He and his men were all killed.

444 The eagle; dancers wore such masks in spiritual ceremonies in the Northwest.

445 25 years, from the end of the US Civil War in 1865 to the end of the cattle boom in the late 1880s.

446 Rodeos, nowadays a big business.

447 Lacrosse, invented by Native Americans and particularly popular in the Southeast.

448 The Winchester rifle, called "the gun that won the West" because it was so popular.

449 Barbed wire, used to protect crops, good pasture, and water, and to keep cattle in.

450 Buffalo Bill; his show toured the United States

and Europe from 1883 to 1916.

451 A "ten-gallon" hat.

452 A saloon.

453 A knife.

454 For food; it was the cook's wagon.

455 At the OK Corral, in Tombstone, Arizona.

Weaponry and War

456 Sideburns (whiskers grown down the sides of the face). Burnside fought in the Civil War.

457 In France; Allied troops landed in northern France to liberate Europe from the Germans.

458 It is a type of curved sword.

459 Crossbows have a longer range, but are slower to reload. They can be deadly at 200 yds (180 m).

460 A backsword, once used by European cavalry.

461 Lead, hence expressions like "a hail of lead."

462 5; they could fire 6 lb (2.7 kg) cannonballs up to 1,100 yards (1,000 m) 2 or 3 times a minute.

463 5 shots; this model was first made in 1862.

464 A musket was a kind of gun.

465 Covered excavations for soldiers to shelter in.

466 A German submarine; U-boat was short for undersea boat.

467 The great general Hannibal (247–182 BC) from the North African city of Carthage.

468 The Battle of Jutland, fought in 1916.

469 Napoleon Bonaparte, who conquered much of Europe, but was finally defeated at the Battle of Waterloo in 1815.

470 Flint, from which the oldest surviving weapons were made.

471 The tank, first used in battle by the British in France in 1916. It was named the tank while being developed, in order to keep what it was a secret.

472 A colonel is the most senior of the 3, and a corporal the least.

473 A sword, felt to have mystical significance.

474 An AK47 is a gun – a Russian rifle.

475 It is a Zulu thrusting spear from South Africa.

476 Grenadiers, in the 1700s; by the 19th century grenadiers were usually just infantry troops.

477 Caltrops were scattered before a battle to lame enemy horses or soldiers who stepped on them.

478 It weighs about 44–55 lb (20–25 kg).

479 Throwing; the multiple blades mean that it can cause damage whichever way it hits.

480 Abraham Lincoln, assassinated in 1865 at the end of the Civil War.

481 Blitzkrieg: from "blitz" meaning lightning and "krieg" meaning war.

482 6 days: it was the Six Day War of 1967 between Israel and several Arab states.

483 The Ethiopian army smashed an Italian invasion at the Battle of Adowa in 1896.

484 The claw of a tiger.

485 It will fly back to you.

486 Genghis Khan: in the 1200s he founded the Mongol Empire that eventually included lands from China to central Europe.

487 North American Indians used tomahawks.

488 A knuckle-duster, worn on the fingers to cause maximum damage when punching people.

489 A division is the biggest, then a brigade, then a regiment, then battalion.

490 It is called no-man's-land.

491 30 years: the Thirty Years War raged across much of Europe from 1618–48. Longer wars, such as the 100

Years War, have not been continuous.

492 It is called a gauntlet.

493 Giuseppe Garibaldi (1807–82), who conquered Sicily and Naples for the new Italy in 1860.

494 Rapiers, which were developed in the 1500s.

495 Jousting, a sport in which knights fought mock battles against each other.

496 It was worn on the wrist. The razor-sharp outer edge is covered in this example.

Clothing

497 Hand spindles were used for spinning and weaving textiles.

498 Louis XIV introduced the wig into the French court, some say to hide his own baldness.

499 Jeans, a US invention, first made in the 1850s.

500 It was used to fasten a belt.

501 China, where they had been used for more than 500 years.

502 In the 18th century. They are made of embroidered muslin; cuffs were also made of lace.

503 Men: in the late 18th century men sometimes hung pouch bags on their belts.

504 In the 1960s, in England.

505 To keep a person cool; fans can also be fashion accessories.

506 The toga, a loose, flowing garment.

507 Headdresses worn by aristocratic women.

508 They were cut into various designs and worn on the face.

509 In the early 20th century.

510 Imperial women wore their hair in elaborate designs, using wigs, hairpieces, and tiaras. They needed hairpins to hold everything in place.

511 In Spain. False bellies were created by tailors with horsehair, rags, or wool.

512 A metal or whalebone framework worn under a dress below the waist to make the dress stick out.

513 Overshoes with platform soles, worn in wet weather. Some platforms reached 30 in (76 cm). They were fashionable during the Renaissance.

514 In the 18th century.

515 Silk, which first reached Europe when two monks smuggled silkworm eggs out of China.

516 The Persians were the first people to cut and fit garments in what is now the European style.

517 The crinoline; it was introduced, in Europe, in 1856, replacing layers of petticoats.

518 France influenced fashions until the outbreak of the French Revolution in 1789.

519 A type of plastic, often used in the form of fibers. Its elastic qualities make it suitable for many types of clothes.

520 A very tall hairstyle, popular in the 1700s.

521 Social etiquette demanded that such upper-class women should keep their hands covered.

522 They were popular in the 1970s.

523 Skirts were first worn above the knee.

524 Both men and women wore platform shoes.

525 Around the ankle; it is an African bracelet.

526 Through the nose; it is a Colombian gold ornament.

527 On the wrist; it is a Pictish bracelet.

528 Probably on the chest; it is an Irish brooch, worn to hold a cloak in place.

529 The ears; these are Thai earrings made from animal skin and painted in gold.

530 Around the neck; it is Zulu necklace.

531 Around the head; it is a headband.

532 Around the waist; it is a gold buckle made from precious stones and worn on a belt.

Inventions: to 1850

533 The hot-air balloon, invented by the Montgolfier brothers in 1783.

534 A pendulum; it made clocks far more accurate.

535 Arches, in Egypt, Iraq, and Pakistan, 4000–3000 bc. The oldest record of a tunnel is in 2180 bc in Iraq.

536 The metric system was standardized in France between 1791 and 1795, the imperial system in England in 1824.

537 The cork; bottle corks later (1670) made the champagne process possible.

538 Gas; it did not become popular for a century.

539 In Europe, in England in 1837; but the first really successful telegraph was made by US inventor Samuel Morse, creator of Morse code, in 1844.

540 Baths, which can be traced back to 2500 BC in Pakistan, and perhaps to 3100 BC in Gaza. Egyptian remains of 1350 BC may be the first shower.

541 The first book was printed in China in AD 868. Movable type was invented about 1040, also in China, and was used to publish a book in 1300.

542 In about 1300, in Italy. Bifocal lenses such as those in the picture were invented in 1784.

543 The violin; it dates to the early 16th century; the first piano was made around 1700, in Italy.

544 In England, in 1509.

545 The steam engine; in 1765 he started to improve Newcomen's design of 1712; in 1784 he invented a steam engine that could turn wheels.

546 He improved maps by inventing a better way of copying the Earth's round surface onto flat paper.

547 The wheelbarrow, invented in China in the 3rd century AD. The lawn mower was invented in 1830.

548 He invented the saxophone.

549 In about 1827, by Joseph-Nicéphore Niépce.

550 Metalworking; it was invented about 7000 BC, perhaps in Turkey, the wheel about 3200 BC in Iraq.

551 It was the first battery.

552 Tarmac, originally called Tarmacadam.

553 The alarm clock; one of the first alarm clocks was used in a monastery in Nuremberg, Germany.

554 *Rocket*; it first ran in 1830 at the start of the railroad boom. The first train ran in 1803.

555 In China, under the Tang dynasty (AD 618–906), although it was not widely used until the 1200s.

556 Concrete was invented by Roman engineers about 200 BC, gunpowder in China around AD 950.

557 In Iraq, about 3500 BC.

558 The electric motor: the first one was built about 1831. The first internal combustion engine was not made until 1859.

559 The bicycle; still known in France as the velo.

560 Postage stamps, first produced in 1840; the first printed Christmas cards were made in 1843.

561 It was the parachute.

562 In Asia: the wheel was used to reel silk in China about AD 1000, and to spin yarn in India soon after.

563 The Etruscans of Italy; they were using false teeth made from animals' teeth in about 700 BC.

564 In China, in AD 105.

The Earth

565 The Pacific is the largest ocean. It covers one-third of the Earth's surface.

566 Asia is the largest continent.

567 Ice; glaciers are like rivers of slowly-moving ice.

568 It is called the mantle.

569 Seismographs measure earthquakes.

570 In Australia; it is called Uluru.

571 Diamond is the hardest mineral.

572 The magnitude of an earthquake.

573 Tsunamis are huge waves set off by undersea earthquakes. Some travel at 490 mph (790 kph).

574 The Earth is 4.6 billion years old.

575 Eclogite is a metamorphic rock – it is formed by the alteration of existing rock. Granite is igneous, formed by the crystallization of molten material.

576 The steeper slopes are called "scarps."

577 Geysers spout hot water.

578 The Himalay; they include the world's highest mountain, Everest, which is 29,078 ft (8,863 m) high.

579 Platinum is the most valuable.

580 The Nile is usually considered the longest, at 4,145 miles (6,670 km) long. The Amazon can be figured as longer because it is 4,195 miles (6,750 km) from its source to the *farthest* of its several mouths.

581 Because it is the only metal that is liquid at room temperature and it is silvery in color.

582 It is 8,100°F (4,500°C).

583 On the shores of the Dead Sea, between Jordan and Israel. It is 1,300 ft (400 m) below sea level.

584 Most land lies in the Northern Hemisphere.

585 Krakatoa, a volcanic island, erupted It was the longest eruption in modern history.

586 Columns of calcite that form underground in caves. Stalagmites grow up from the floor and stalactites grow down from the roof.

587 Rocks.

588 Water.

Astronomy

589 The planet Venus.

590 Mercury and Venus.

591 The Milky Way.

592 The Sun.

593 "The cow jumped over the Moon."

594 It is Jupiter.

595 Time is the fourth dimension; modern science sees space and time as a unity, called "spacetime."

596 The dark patches are flat areas. The lighter patches are mountains.

597 Albert Einstein.

598 Olympus Mons, 3 times as high as Everest.

599 Galileo; with his telescope he discovered Jupiter's satellites, and craters on the Moon.

600 There are 687 Earth days in a year on Mars.

601 He orbited the Earth.

602 A comet, Halley's Comet.

603 In space, it orbits around the Earth.

604 The film *Star Wars*.

605 Russian; Valentina Tereshkova, in 1963.

606 Pluto, which was not found until 1930. It is also the farthest away from the Sun.

607 Mars; from Earth it looks like a red disk.

608 Russian; called *Salyut 1*, it was launched in 1971.

609 It is called "the Big Bang."

610 He discovered the force of gravity.

The Human Body

611 100,000 times each day.

612 A child; children have about 300 more bones than adults. In adults, bones fuse together.

613 Tooth enamel is the hardest substance.

614 5 pints (3 liters) of air.

615 China; in 1989 there were reported to be 61,929.

616 Keratin is found in nails, hair, and skin.

617 A baby develops in the uterus, or womb.

618 The skin is the largest organ.

619 Sigmund Freud; he treated patients by listening to them talk about their dreams and thoughts.

620 The ribcage protects the chest organs.

621 It can only bend forward and backward.

622 The small intestine, measuring 21 ft (6.5 m). The large intestine is 6 ft (1.8 m) long. It is thicker.

623 More than 600 muscles.

624 This is true.

625 In 1895.

626 In the spine.

627 The head weighs about 8.8 lb (4 kg).

628 In the 19th century.

629 They are made up of proteins.

630 A gastroscope is used to examine the stomach.

631 The femur; it is found in the thigh.

632 Louis Pasteur; he led the way for the development of antiseptic surgery.

633 206, over half of them are in the hands and feet.

634 Marie Curie.

635 A local anesthetic numbs a part of the body. A general anesthetic makes a patient unconscious.

636 Alexander Fleming, in 1928.

637 To carry blood from the heart around the body.

638 Doctors believed that too much blood in the body was a cause of disease.

639 In 1849. Elizabeth Blackwell was accepted into medical school in 1847.

640 It was forbidden by the church to dissect bodies for scientific study.

641 Amputated shattered limbs.

642 The major blood groups are A, B, AB, and O.

643 More than 200 muscles.

644 This form of medicine is called acupuncture.

645 Louise Brown was born in England in 1978.

646 In the ear; it is called the stirrup.

647 It was performed in 1967.

648 In the 19th century.

649 Bile aids digestion.

650 A midwife delivers babies.

651 A stethoscope listens to the heart and lungs.

652 In 1853; devised by Charles Plavaz in France.

653 There are 27 bones in the hand.

654 It was set up in 1948 to act as an information center concerning health problems facing the world.

655 They are attached to the sternum or breastbone.

656 They are sight, smell, taste, hearing, and touch.

657 When we are cold, tiny muscles lift the body hairs to trap warm air.

658 They were introduced in the 1840s. Patients became unconscious by inhaling nitrous oxide, ether, or chloroform.

Biology and Chemistry

659 It turns pink or red.

660 DNA contains this information.

661 Water, made of hydrogen (H) and oxygen (O).

662 Light; there is a prism inside the scope that splits a light beam into its spectrum, that is, its different colors, or wavelengths.

663 It separates mixtures by boiling and condensing them.

664 Pigs' bladders were used in the 1700s to hold gases before glass equipment was introduced.

665 DNA, the chemical from which chromosomes, "the building blocks of life," are made.

666 It is known as laughing gas.

667 It is a gas generator; P. J. Kipp introduced it in 1862 to provide the gas hydrogen sulfide.

668 It helps the skin to tan.

669 A virus; the model pictured shows the virus injecting its DNA into a cell.

670 Salt; sodium chloride is its scientific name.

671 An element is a substance that cannot be broken down into simpler substances.

672 The chemical elements. There are more than 100.

673 Glass, probably first made in Egypt, 3000 BC.

674 It is designed to measure the purity of air.

675 Hydrogen is the lightest element.

676 Genes; inherited characteristics are passed down the generations in the genes.

677 Water, air, and sunlight to grow properly.

678 It is acidic, so can be relieved by applying cold water containing some bicarbonate of soda, which is alkaline. A wasp sting is alkaline; it is treated with a teaspoon of vinegar, an acid, in half a glass of water.

679 They were called alchemists.

680 Romantic love; this is an unscientific use of the word chemistry.

Weather and Climate

681 Clouds; cumulus clouds are rounded clouds with flattish bases.

682 Antarctica; the central plateau is a cold desert. It is the windiest continent.

683 Aztec, it is the Aztec Sun god, Tonatuich.

684 Low or falling pressure often indicates rain.

685 Air pressure, to help forecast weather.

686 It warms us up; heat trapped by gases in the lower atmosphere keeps the Earth warm. Pollution is increasing the amount of "greenhouse gases" in the atmosphere, and heating the Earth too much.

687 Wind speed; most weather stations use them.

688 Nitrogen; it is 78% nitrogen and 21% oxygen.

689 Rainbows form when the Sun breaks through the clouds after rain and light is reflected in raindrops still falling on the opposite side of the sky.

690 In Antarctica; the coldest temperature ever recorded there was −128.6°F (−89.2°C).

691 An aneroid barometer; in the drum is a vacuum that expands or contracts as air pressure changes.

692 The fog forms as warm, moist, Californian air blows over the cool Pacific ocean currents.

693 Bands of red, green, or yellow light that move across the night sky in northern polar regions.

694 Lightest; the eye of a hurricane is calm.

695 The time of day; the moving shadow cast on the dial by the needle shows what time it is.

696 The troposphere; all that we call weather happens in the troposphere.

697 Hawaii; it is Mount Wai-'ale-'ale in Hawaii.

698 The ozone layer, which shields the Earth from the Sun's ultraviolet rays.

699 The side the clouds come from (the windward side); the farther side (the leeward side) is drier.

700 No; you see the lightning first.

701 They create wind, as air rushes from areas of high pressure to areas of lower pressure.

702 The Earth's rotation; the Coriolis effect describes how this rotation deflects the winds of the world.

703 Hot air rises.

704 Yes.

705 In Africa; the temperature at Dallol in Ethiopia averages 94°F (34°C).

Inventions: 1850–1950

706 They were the first to fly an airplane.

707 The fax machine; an early form of fax machine called the pantelegraph was installed in France in 1856. The telephone was not invented until 1876.

708 It played for 23 minutes.

709 It was introduced in 1920.

710 Pneumatic (inflatable) tires. They had been invented in 1845 and "reinvented" in 1888, but the Michelins were first to make them for cars, in 1895.

711 The meter; it was not quite new to the world, for the ancient Romans fitted a kind of meter to carts.

712 The Model T Ford; the assembly line had earlier been used to make clocks and watches.

713 Germany; Karl Benz made a motorized tricycle in 1885 and had built a 4-wheel car by 1893.

714 Germany; it opened in Berlin.

715 About 1930, in the United States.

716 The gramophone, an early kind of record player.

717 In 1885, by Gottlieb Daimler in Germany.

718 The helicopter; the first practical helicopter was built in 1936, the first jet airplane in 1939.

719 He invented it in 1938.

720 The airship, in 1852. The first glider flew in 1853, but controlled flight in a glider waited until 1891. The airplane first flew in 1903.

721 In London, England.

722 30 tons.

723 In 1920, in Pittsburgh, Pennsylvania.

724 It had a red light and a green light. Yellow came 4 years later.

725 Thomas Edison was American.

726 The cash register.

727 In 1926, invented by John Logie Baird.

728 False; the first practical lightbulb was invented in 1879, the electric iron in 1882.

729 In 1872; chewing gum was an old Native American idea.

730 In 1946, but microwaves in the home did not appear until 1955.

731 Guglielmo Marconi; in 1894 he was sending radio waves across the room, and by 1901 he was sending messages across the Atlantic.

732 It was invented in 1857.

733 It only played 1 tune.

734 Coca-Cola, launched as "the esteemed brain tonic and intellectual beverage."

735 Tuned into a radio broadcast.

736 On a squash court in Chicago, in the United States, in 1942.

737 It recorded and reproduced sound.

738 In 1950, for use in restaurants.

739 The ballpoint pen.

740 In 1914, called the "hookless fastener."

741 The electric refrigerator.

The Modern World

742 Nothing; not even light can escape a black hole.

743 Heat itself; self-heating canned food was invented in 1991.

744 PC stands for personal computer.

745 Cable; it transmits TV down fiber-optic cables.

746 There were about 537 million.

747 Videotape, in 1956; microchips – integrated electronic circuits printed on a single silicon chip – invented in 1959, have made computers far faster.

748 The first electric toothbrush.

749 Very low temperature; some substances lose almost all resistance to electricity at low temperature.

750 Light, laser light carrying vision, sound, etc., in the form of data.

751 A laser beam, directed onto the bomb's target.

752 A cassette player, with headphones, small enough to be worn.

753 Pacemakers help the heart beat regularly.

754 In 1982, in Utah.

755 A floppy disk; a flexible magnetic disk that stores information.

756 3-dimensional holograms, made in 1965. Personal computers arrived in 1975, but the first successful PC was not produced until 1978.

757 A mouse; moving it moves a pointer on screen.

758 The scanning tunneling microscope, invented in 1981, can magnify objects 100 million times.

759 Their ability to take off and land vertically.

760 A computer.

761 In 1972, in the United States.

762 A fax is a document transmitted down a telephone line.

763 A credit card incorporating a computer chip.

764 The United States; Japan produces half as much.

765 The food processor, able to mix, chop, or slice.

766 Click on it; a mouse controls a pointer that can be used to activate functions of a computer by clicking on icons, without using the keyboard.

767 Fission splits atoms, releasing energy; fusion combines them, releasing even more energy.

768 The cassette tape recorder.

769 400 million instructions per second.

770 Cruise missiles, a US innovation.

771 The industrial robot, in 1962; the first digital watch was made in 1971.

772 The most accurate clocks are atomic.

773 By our DNA; we each have a unique pattern.

774 The hovercraft.

775 In 1981; it was the first reusable space launcher.

776 The Concorde, a joint English-French project.

777 It is a liquid crystal display, or LCD for short.

778 *Sputnik* was the first space satellite, launched by the Soviet Union in 1957.

779 Electricity; wind is used to drive wind turbines.

780 The L.A.S.E.R., that is, the Laser.

781 CD stands for Compact Disc.

782 Rubik's Cube, a brain-teasing puzzle.

783 Reduce pollution from car exhausts.

784 A device to link computers via a telephone line.

785 Computers; CD-ROMs store information.

786 A hydrometer to measure the density of liquids.

787 A spring balance for measuring weight.

788 A test tube.

789 A Bunsen burner.

790 A pipette.

791 A micrometer for measuring small objects.

Soccer

792 A soccer match lasts for 90 minutes.

793 It was held in Mexico.

794 Just over 17 hours; this feat was achieved by Huh Nam Jin of South Korea..

795 On the shin, to protect against bruises and cuts.

796 On the streets; there were no time limits and few rules.

797 Brazil; they have won the World Cup 4 times.

798 It weighs 8 oz (250 g).

799 A team consists of 11 players and 3 substitutes.

800 The goalkeeper.

801 A linesman; linesmen use flags to indicate when a player fouls or the ball goes out of play.

802 An overhead kick in which the player back flips to direct the ball behind him.

803 To draw attention to fouls.

804 The chest, head, and thighs.

805 At kickoffs and penalties.

806 The team captain, for identification.

807 140 play at the international level.

808 5 shots for each side.

809 Italy won the World Cup in 1982.

810 It is made of leather.

811 Pelé, who said "make the ball your friend."

812 A kick in which the goalkeeper gathers the ball, drops it, and kicks it before it can hit the ground.

813 Ireland plays Gaelic soccer.

814 A red card; a yellow card is a lesser penalty.

815 Fédération Internationale de Football Association; it is soccer's ruling body.

816 England beat Australia 17–0 in 1951. (This match was a "friendly" and not a full international.)

817 Geoff Hurst; England beat West Germany 4–2.

818 Luciano Pavarotti sang *Nessun Dorma*, which became the theme tune for the 1990 World Cup.

819 In the penalty area.

820 To give them a better grip of the ball.

821 Cameroon.

Indoor Sports

822 Boxing; Queensberry rules were laid down by the English Marquess of Queensberry in 1865.

823 In poker; it is made up of the Ace, King, Queen, Jack, and 10 of a single suit.

824 Garry Kasparov, who won in 1985, aged 22.

825 Sumo, usually the province of large, bulky men.

826 Racing pigeons, which fly vast distances home.

827 Ice hockey. Players hit a puck (a hard rubber disk), the goaltender defends the goal, and players have to spend time off the ice in the "sin bin," or penalty box, when they break the rules.

828 Tenpin bowling: the players added a 10th pin to the 9 with which they had played skittles and arranged them in a triangle instead of a diamond.

829 Gymnastics, which also involves floor exercises.

830 Organic materials, that is, pieces of bone or wood, tied around shoes. Metal blades were first used in the 1600s.

831 Chess; to lose your king is to lose the game, so the king must be protected.

832 Libyan Suleiman Ali Nashaush was 8 ft (2.45 m) tall.

833 The "clean and jerk" is easier: the bar is first lifted onto the chest, then the lifter steadies himself, then lifts it over his head. In the "snatch" the bar is lifted above the head in one movement.

834 They are marbles teams from Britain. Marbles is a game played by flicking marbles at each other.

835 Karaoke; it involves singing along to a prerecorded tune.

836 Rocky Marciano; Muhammad Ali lost several, but came back to be world champion three times.

837 When the direct path from the cue ball to the object ball is blocked by another ball.

838 No one has ever dribbled more than 4 at a time.

839 Pool, or at least the "8-ball" version of the game.

Outdoor Sports

840 Polo fields, which cover 12.4 acres (5 hectares).

841 In cricket: an over is a set of six deliveries (deliveries are roughly like pitches in baseball). If no runs are scored in it, it is called a maiden over.

842 Boris Becker, youngest ever men's champion.

843 In cricket, it is taking 3 wickets in 3 balls. The reason for the name is that in the early days of cricket, bowlers who did this were given a top hat. In other sports, a hat-trick is 3 goals in the same game.

844 A ground stroke is played after the ball has bounced, a volley is played before it bounces.

845 Golf. A birdie is a hole played 1 stroke under par; an eagle is 2 under; and a bogey is 1 above.

846 A log, which is called a caber.

847 In soccer.

848 A football; the other two are round.

849 In football.

850 A very large diamond; the bases are arranged in a diamond shape.

851 Tennis: "love," "deuce," and "advantage" are different tennis scores.

852 He was 98 years old; the oldest woman was 82.

853 England. The English invented soccer, rugby, cricket, tennis, squash, and other games.

854 In cricket. This is one of the ways in which a batsman can get out. The inning ends when 10 of the 11 batsmen on a team are out.

855 Formula 1 is the fastest of these three divisions of motor racing.

The Olympic Games

856 There are 5 rings.

857 They represent the 5 continents.

858 Bronze; people who finish second are awarded silver medals.

859 The photo-finish: pictures of the finish are looked at very closely.

860 It was Nadia Comaneci.

861 They go over backward.

862 Ski jumping; they jump from these two hills.

863 He was disqualified for taking illegal drugs.

864 Every 4 years.

865 The marathon is the longest distance run, although competitors such as the walkers and cross-country (Nordic) skiers race over longer distances.

866 The pommel horse is a key bit of gymnastic equipment; originally created to help soldiers learn riding skills, it is a leather-covered shape with two pommels (handles) along its upper surface.

867 It was in Greece. Only men could compete. Women had their own separate games.

868 US swimmer Mark Spitz won 7 gold medals in 1972. 4 were individual medals and 3 were team golds. US speed skater Eric Heiden, who won 5 golds at the 1980 Winter Olympics, holds the record for individual golds won in a single games.

869 The relays; 4 runners race 100 meters each or 400 meters each, passing a baton between them.

870 There are 10 events: 100 meter, long jump, shot put, high jump, 400 meter, 110 meter hurdles, discus, pole vault, javelin, and 1,500 meter.

871 The men's pentathlon. The women's pentathlon consisted of the 100 meter hurdles, shot put, high jump, long jump, and the 200 meter until 1984, when the javelin and 800 meter were added and the event became the heptathlon.

872 The sport is called rhythmic gymnastics.

873 Adolf Hitler; he refused to present black US athlete Jesse Owens with the 4 golds he had won.

874 The competitors stand. In rifle-shooting competitions they usually lie down.

875 The discus can be thrown 3 times as far.

876 There are 9 people in an "eight": 8 rowers and the cox, who steers and dictates the pace.

877 The record is 10 gold medals, won by Raymond Clarence Ewry of the United States, between 1900 and 1908, in the standing high, long, and triple jumps.

878 Yes; amateur boxers do; professionals don't.

879 The third element is a hop.

880 The downhill; in the other two the competitors have to follow a twisting course marked out with flags. In the downhill, they ski straight down.

881 It featured sprinters in the 1924 Olympics.

882 A skater; the German figure skater Katarina Witt received them after winning the gold in 1984.

883 It was 40 years, achieved by 4 contestants, 3 in yachting and 1 in fencing.

884 A low score, because points are awarded for faults; as in golf, the lowest scorer wins. Only 3 people have won the Olympic show jumping competition without any faults at all.

885 The other sport is rifle shooting.

886 Freestyle is the fastest swimming style, followed by butterfly, then backstroke, then breaststroke.

887 They hit a touch-sensitive board at the end of the swimming pool.

888 The javelin can be thrown slightly farther.

889 The steeplechase, run over 3,000 meters.

890 In the Olympic "village."

891 The Olympic flame, or Olympic torch. It is kept burning always at Olympia in Greece, and a torch is carried by runners to each Olympics, where it is used to light a giant torch at the opening ceremony.

892 In synchronized swimming, now an Olympic sport.

893 The ice dancers; ice dance is one of the skating events.

894 Bodybuilding is the odd one out.

895 In 1896, in Athens.

896 There were 169 nations represented.

897 Sydney won, and will host the Olympics.

898 It is one of the riding competitions.

899 Trick question: the Olympics did not take place in 1944 because World War II was being fought at the time.

Art and Architecture

900 They design buildings.

901 An artisan is a craftsperson, or a skilled worker; an artist is a person skilled in an art such as painting or drawing.

902 On the roof; they are different types of domes.

903 In the 20th century, between 1929 and 1931.

904 Water; aqua is Latin for water.

905 Many painters use oil paints; other types of paint used include watercolors.

906 In Sydney. It was designed by Danish architect Jørn Utzon.

907 Gargoyles.

908 Sculptors make statues and carve wood, stone, and other materials in 3 dimensions.

909 Columns; all these styles originated in ancient Greece.

910 Expressionism, an early 20th-century artistic movement that aimed to express emotion, rather than to show reality in a natural way.

911 Green; the three primary colors of paint are yellow, blue, and red. All other colors of paint can be made by mixing these 3 colors.

912 Mosaic; mosaics are often found in churches, palaces, or great houses.

913 Going to a class in which they will draw someone or something from life.

914 Clay, a sturdy material for building.

915 No, Gothic arches are pointed and Norman arches are rounded.

916 Skyscrapers; the first was built in Chicago, Illinois, in 1883.

917 Sable. Sable martens are small, carnivorous mammals, and the brushes are made from their fur.

Dance

918 In the 19th century; Marie Taglioni first danced on pointe in *La Sylphide* in 1832.

919 There are 5.

920 The waltz, first danced in Vienna, Austria.

921 *Fame*, set in New York City.

922 Moira Shearer starred in *The Red Shoes*.

923 The leotard, a close-fitting one-piece garment covering the torso.

924 Fred Astaire and Ginger Rogers; they starred in 10 films together.

925 *Saturday Night Fever*.

926 Flamenco; dancers hold their heads up high as they stamp their feet and turn around.

927 Breakdancing; some dancers could spin on their heads.

928 Layers of satin, paper, and a coarse material called burlap glued together.

929 Vogueing, in which dancers imitate the poses of catwalk models.

930 The pavlova, a kind of meringue cake, was named after Russian ballerina Anna Pavlova.

931 Louis XIV; he was an avid dancer.

932 A tutu.

933 Gene Kelly; he starred in the hit musical *Singin' in the Rain*.

934 *Starlight Express*, by Andrew Lloyd Webber.

935 The choreographer.

936 In North America.

Music

937 They all belong to the saxophone family.

938 Giuseppe Verdi; the first performance was part of the celebrations for the opening of the Suez Canal, in 1869 in Egypt.

939 Bing Crosby; his recording of *White Christmas* in 1942 is the biggest-selling record of all time.

940 A double bass is the biggest of them.

941 They are all famous opera singers.

942 They are all operas written by Wolfgang Amadeus Mozart.

943 A conductor; his or her job is to direct the band or orchestra.

944 The brass family.

945 Elvis Presley; he is known as "The King."

946 The *Messiah*.

947 Baroque.

948 Peter Ilyich Tchaikovsky.

949 In 1597, by the Italian Jacopo Peri. It was called *Dafne* and was performed in Florence.

950 John Lennon and Paul McCartney.

951 There are 88 keys.

952 Bob Dylan; his real name is Robert Allen Zimmerman.

953 Louis Armstrong; he devised the first solo style in jazz with his daring improvisations.

954 An orchestra; 200 years ago orchestras were 30-strong, but some music of the late 19th century and 20th century requires more than 100 musicians.

955 A sitar; this one has 7 main strings that pass over arched metal frets.

956 The harp; it is a very difficult instrument to play. While plucking 47 strings with the fingertips the harpist must work 7 foot pedals.

957 Bob Marley; his group was called the Wailers.

958 Abba; they went on to make 13 hit albums.

959 2 violins, a viola, and a cello.

960 The player blows air into it through a nostril. It is called a nose flute.

961 You blow through it, and it makes a deep, resonant sound; it is an Aboriginal instrument.

962 A tambourine; a dancer taps it with the fingers and shakes it or bangs it against the body.

963 It can produce voices, sound effects, and new sounds never heard before.

964 Shake it.

965 *Hair*; it opened the day after the abolition of British stage censorship.

966 *West Side Story* by Leonard Bernstein.

967 1970.

Movies, TV, and Theater

968 90 ft (27 m); a full-length feature film uses 1.5 miles (2.5 km) of film.

969 2; Johnny Weismuller, who won 3 gold medals in 1924 and 2 in 1928, and Buster Crabbe, who won 1 gold in 1932.

970 William Shakespeare, England's greatest playwright, who wrote nearly 40 plays between about 1588 and 1613.

971 Someone who watches too much television; it is a rather rude term, suggesting that they sit in front of the television like a vegetable, not thinking much.

972 Walt Disney, the most famous creator of animated films in history.

973 Britain; the BBC (British Broadcasting Corporation) began regular service in 1936.

974 Because the images it shot were recorded onto three films at once, recording red, blue, and green individually. A special printing process then put the colors back together.

975 Tragedy; both comedy and tragedy were first developed, in theatrical terms, in ancient Athens.

976 The soccer World Cup; the Olympics have perhaps 2.5 billion viewers in all, while the total audience for all the World Cup soccer games may add up to an audience of about 25 billion.

977 It was the first "talkie," the first feature film that featured sound. Most of it was still silent, however. The first all-talking film came in 1929.

978 In a theater; the boxes are at the side, with very good views, and the stalls are the lowest seats. The tier is above them and the upper tier above that.

979 A screenplay, written by a scriptwriter.

980 In ancient Greece; Athens saw the first plays that were like the plays we see today. Many of those 2,500-year-old Athenian plays are still performed.

981 Sherlock Holmes, who has appeared in over 200 films to date. Dracula has featured in over 150.

982 The first satellite broadcasting service was launched.

983 24; an average 90-minute feature film is made up of about 130,000 separate frames.

984 A moving image; when it was rotated very fast, the painted images seemed to become a single moving image on the screen. It was created in England in the 1870s.

985 A miniaturized TV.

986 Hollywood.

987 Steven Spielberg; George Lucas has produced, among other films, the Star Wars series (he also directed the first one) and *Raiders of the Lost Ark*.

988 25 times a second is standard. John Logie Baird's 1926 television sets projected a new image 10 times a second.

989 A microphone; the boom is the long pole on which the microphone is placed so that it can be held above the actor's head. When a camera is placed on a boom, the person operating it is known as a boom man or woman.

990 The sound of someone's arm or leg being chopped off.

991 In France, by the Pathé company, which also built projectors and made newsreel films.

992 "Cut!" When directors want to start filming, they say "Action!"

993 India, where more than 900 feature-length films have been produced in a single year.

994 China, which has recorded over 20 billion movie theater attendances in a single year.

995 *Ben Hur*, produced in 1959, starring Charlton Heston in the title role.

996 A hero turtle, from the 1990 film *Teenage Mutant Ninja Turtles*.

997 Dracula, star of vampire movies since 1921.

998 Charlie Chaplin, the great star of silent comedy, wore them in the film *The Immigrant*.

999 Marilyn Monroe, who wore this dress in the film *Some Like it Hot*.

1000 A gremlin from the film *Gremlins*.

1001 The Pink Panther, symbol of the Pink Panther films, and star of a series of TV cartoons.

Index

Acknowledgments

Dorling Kindersley would like to thank:

Peter Anderson, Geoff Brightling, Jane Burton, Peter Chadwick, Andy Crawford, Geoff Dann, Philip Dowell, Mike Dunning, Lynton Gardiner, Phillip Gatward, John Garrett, Christi Graham, Frank Greenaway, Peter Hayman, Chas Howson, Colin Keates, Dave King, Liz McAulay, Andrew McRobb, Ray Moller, Nick Nicholls, Stephen Oliver, Roger Phillips, Karl Shone, James Stevenson, Clive Streeter, Harry Taylor, Kim Taylor, Matthew Ward, Jerry Young, and Michel Zabé, for special photography.

The American Museum of Natural History, Arbour Antiques in New York, Ashmolean Museum, Birmingham City Museum, Cambridge Museum, Charles Darwin Museum, INAH.-CNCA, Mexico, Museum of London,

Museum of the Moving Image, Natural History Museum, National Maritime Museum, Pitt Rivers Museum, Royal Pavilion, Art Gallery and Museum, Brighton, Smithsonian Institution in Washington D.C., Trustees of the National Museums of Scotland (Scottish United Services Museum), National Railway Museum, Shakespeare Globe Trust, Sir John Soane's Museum, St Bride Printing Library, Trustees of the University Museum of Archaeology and Anthropology, Wallace Collection, Warwick Castle, Worthing Museum and Art Gallery.

Djinn von Noorden for editorial assistance and Ivan Finnegan for design assistance.
Gillian Denton, Claire Gillard, and Phil Wilkinson for help with the leisure section.
Ingrid Nilsson for picture research.
Marion Dent for the index.

Picture credits
t top, *b* below, *c* center, *l* left, *r* right.
American Museum of Natural History 27c; Ashmolean Museum 24tl, 31cb; Birmingham City Museum 26br; Bolton Museum 18tl; Bridgeman Art Library/Nasjonalgallertiet, Oslo 50tr; British Museum 18tr, 19tl, 20tl, c, tr, cr, bl, 21tl, bl, br; Cambridge Museum 31cra; Charles Darwin Museum 25tr; Ermine Street Guard 21tr; Werner Forman Archive 39tl; Glasgow Museum 40tl; Ronald Grant Archive 55bc (box); Jim Henson's Creature Shop 55bl (box); Michael Holford 11cr; Image Bank 49br; INAH Mexican Museum Authority 26c, tr, cl; Ligabue Studies and Researchers, Venice/Erizzo Editrice 4/5c; Museum of London 22tc, 30tl; Museum of the Moving Image 54tl, 55cr (box), 55tcl, c/Jim Henson's Creature Shop 55bl (box); NASA 35c, 43b; National Motor Museum, Beaulieu 40b;

National Maritime Museum 25tl, 25tc, 25c, 25cl, 35bl; National Museum of Scotland 31cl, 31cla; National Railway Museum, York 32/3b; Natural History Museum 12tr, 13c, 34br, 34tr; Florence Nightingale Museum 36c; Liberto Perugi 36tl, br; © Renault 47c; Pitt Rivers 29tl, br, bl, 31ca, car, tcb, tc; Royal Museum of Scotland 26bl; Science Museum 54c; Smithsonian Institute 37r, br, 40cr, 41br, cr, 43cb; Sir John Soane's Museum 50bl; Wallace Collection 23tc, 24bl; Warwick Castle 28c; Robin Wigington, Arbour Antiques 28br; Worthing Art Gallery and Museum 31br.

Every effort has been made to trace the copyright holders and we apologize in advance for any unintentional omissions. We would be pleased to insert the appropriate acknowledgment in any subsequent edition of this publication.